**Making Headway**
Pre-Intermediate

# Everyday Listening and Speaking

**Making Headway**
Pre-Intermediate

# Everyday Listening and Speaking

Sarah Cunningham
Peter Moor

**Oxford University Press**

Oxford University Press
Walton Street, Oxford OX2 6DP

Oxford New York Toronto Madrid
Delhi Bombay Calcutta Madras Karachi
Kuala Lumpur Singapore Hong Kong
Tokyo Nairobi Dar es Salaam Cape Town
Melbourne Auckland

and associated companies in
Berlin Ibadan

ISBN 0 19 435500 4

Typeset by Tradespools Ltd, Frome, Somerset

Printed in Malta by Interprint Limited

**Acknowledgements**
The authors would like to thank the Series
editors, John and Liz Soars, for their
invaluable input and advice.

*Illustrations by*
David Murray
Nigel Paige

*Location photography by*
Emily Andersen

*Studio photography by*
Mark Mason

The publishers would like to thank the
following for permission to reproduce
photographs:
The Aviation Picture Library
Robert Harding Picture Library
The Image Bank

The publishers would also like to thank the
following for their participation in location
photography and for the use of their
premises:

Eckersley School of English, Oxford
The High Health Club, Oxford
The Holly Bush, London
Notting Hill Police Station, London
Portobello Car Hire, London
Trailfinders, London

# Contents

# Foreword

*Everyday Listening and Speaking*

Language skills rarely exist in isolation. We often write in reaction to something we have read, just as we often comment on what we have heard on the radio or seen on the television. The skills of listening and speaking are probably the ones given most prominence in the modern language classroom as they are the skills of everyday interaction and, as such, they are completely interdependent. When meeting people for the first time, hiring a car, or going to the bank, it is not enough for language users to know what they themselves want to say. They must react to the situation and to the language they are confronted with, and then amend their response accordingly.

Class time provides the opportunity to rehearse how the foreign language is used in the real world. This book develops the two skills of listening and speaking in a highly systematic and practical manner. The authors have carefully selected a range of situations that visitors to an English-speaking country could well find themselves in. The better these can be practised in advance, the more successful the learners' actual performance will be.

Students' interest will be engaged by the practicality of the topics. We feel sure they will find the tasks relevant, challenging, and enjoyable. New language is presented and contextualized, and known language is developed via the extensive practice activities.

Teachers of lower levels are constantly looking out for ways of engaging their students in fluent conversation; interesting listening material based on everyday situations is also much appreciated. This book provides both. Teachers can select a topic which is appropriate to their class, and they will be able to rely on the material to provide a thorough, balanced lesson or series of lessons.

John and Liz Soars
*Series editors*

# Introduction

**Who this book is for**

**Students** This book is for young adults at pre-intermediate level who want to use English to travel and would like to practise the type of language they will meet in real, everyday situations.

**Teachers** This book is for teachers using *Headway Pre-Intermediate* or any other pre-intermediate course. It provides additional listening material which links in smoothly with popular themes like health, travel, or leisure.

**How the book is organized**

Each of the fifteen units takes about one to one and a half hours of class time. The main focus of each unit is a taped conversation or conversations, and listening and speaking are practised equally.

Each unit is divided into four parts:

**Before you listen** This creates interest in the topic and prepares the student for key vocabulary and culture-specific expressions.

**Listening for information** provides tasks aimed at general comprehension or comprehension of specific information in the text. The students are not expected or encouraged to follow every word of the conversation. Often they are expected to listen to a conversation more than once and are given a different task each time they listen. This develops confidence and helps them to build up a fuller understanding of the text.

**Listening for language** This gives intensive listening practice by focusing on short extracts from the conversations in more detail. As well as helping to improve listening skills, these activities draw the students' attention to useful expressions and structures which they are then encouraged to practise in preparation for the **Speaking** activity.

**Speaking** Through roleplay activities, the students act out some of the situations they have encountered in the listenings, and may encounter in real life. They provide the opportunity to use in context language that has been isolated in the unit. The activities are structured in a variety of ways, encouraging the students to use the language creatively, while providing clear guidance and ideas to stimulate the imagination.

The tapescripts and answer key at the end of this book help the teacher and allow the students to use the book independently.

**How to use the book**

Most activities in the book are self-explanatory. However, here are a few general hints to help the teacher and the students.

**To the teacher**

1 It is important to prepare the students for the topic before a listening, so it is not advisable to omit the first section. But if time is short, the discussion questions in this section can be dealt with very briefly.

2 It is a good idea to focus the students on the first task or questions *before* playing the tape, as this gives the initial listening far greater purpose.

3 If the students find the listenings difficult, it may be necessary to replay the tape several times. In the long-term, however, it is better training for the students' listening skills if you play the texts all the way through, rather than stopping at the answer to each question.

4 If time is short, the activities in the **Listening for language** section could be omitted. However, they do pre-teach useful items for the **Speaking** activities at the end of each unit, and provide a good opportunity for you to correct pronunciation, etc.

5 The rolecards, questions, etc. in the **Speaking** section are invaluable in preparing the students to speak, so give them enough time to prepare.

6 It is important for pre-intermediate students' confidence to have the opportunity to express themselves in English, even if they make a lot of mistakes. This will be easier if you keep a low profile at the **Speaking** stage, and do not correct too much.

7 Try to do the activities in the order given, as they are intended to build up the students' confidence and understanding systematically.

**To the student working independently**

1 Even if you cannot discuss the questions in the **Before you listen** section with another student, read them and think about them, as this will help you to understand the conversations on the tape better.

2 Read the questions in the **Listening for information** section *before* you listen to the tape and *only* try to answer these questions. You do not need to understand every word on the tape!

3 Try to listen to the whole conversation. Don't stop the tape after every few words. In real life, you usually can't 'stop the tape'!

4 You may want to read the tapescripts at the back of the book. But try to do this *after* you have finished the listening tasks.

5 After you have done the **Listening for language** activities, you could *record* yourself and compare your pronunciation to that on the tape.

6 If you can, find a friend to do the **Speaking** activities with. If not, write or act out the conversation by yourself!

# Nice to meet you

**Before you listen**

Look at the picture of the two people below. Where are they? What are they doing? Do you think they know each other? What can you say about them from what you see?

**Listening for information**

T.1a

**1** You're travelling from London to Paris on the same train as these two people. They start talking. You love listening to other people's conversations! Listen to the first part of their conversation. How much of the table below can you complete? Compare answers with a partner

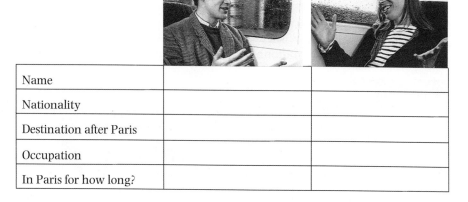

| Name | | |
|---|---|---|
| Nationality | | |
| Destination after Paris | | |
| Occupation | | |
| In Paris for how long? | | |

T.1b

**2** Listen to the second part of their conversation. Can you complete the rest of the table? Compare answers with your partner.

**Listening for language**

**1** In A and B below, there are some sentences from Marc and Maree's conversation. In each sentence, write in the missing word from this box.

| are | introduced | days | meet | do | nice | French |
|-----|-----------|------|------|-----|------|--------|
| teacher | from | where | staying | would | | |

**A**

1 _____ are you from – England?

2 Are you _____ in Paris?

3 _____ you from Paris?

4 What _____ you do?

5 I'm sorry, I haven't _____ myself. My name's Marc.

6 _____ you like to come and have some breakfast?

**B**

No, actually. I'm _____ Australia.

Just for two or three _____ .

No, no. I'm not _____ .

I'm a _____ . I teach small children in a primary school.

Nice to _____ you, Marc.

Breakfast? Oh, yes! That would be _____ .

◀ T.1a/b  ⌐○ **2** Now listen to Marc and Maree's conversation again and check your answers.

**Speaking**

**1** Work alone. Choose one of the people below. Give him/her a name, a nationality, and an occupation, and invent some other information.

**2** Work with a partner, but don't tell your partner which character you chose. Together, choose one of the places below. Decide where you are travelling to and from.

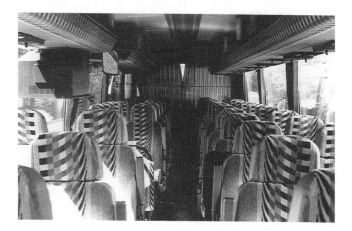

**3** One of you starts the conversation by asking a question.

Example
*Excuse me. Where / When / What / Why …*

Find out as much as you can about the other person: name, nationality, occupation, reason for travelling, etc. Try to keep the conversation going as long as possible.

**4** Now can you guess which character your partner was? What did you find out about him / her?

# 2 In the air

**1** How do you feel about flying? Work with a partner and answer the questions below.

– How often do you travel by plane?
*Never / Less than twice a year / More than twice a year.*
– What do you like most about flying?
– Is there anything you don't like about it?
– When you fly, do you usually feel worried/relaxed/excited/bored?

**2** Here are some of the things that normally happen when you travel by plane. Do they happen *before you fly* (B), *after you fly* (A), or *on the aeroplane* (O)? Put the correct letter in each box below. (In some cases, more than one letter is possible.)

|  |  |
|---|---|
| ❑ **1** You have a meal. | ❑ **6** You watch a video. |
| ❑ **2** You go through customs. | ❑ **7** You show your passport. |
| ❑ **3** You get off the plane. | ❑ **8** You land. |
| ❑ **4** You check in your baggage. | ❑ **9** You fasten your seat-belt. |
| ❑ **5** You take off. | ❑ **10** You collect your baggage. |

**Listening for information**

**T.2a**

Two passengers are on Flight IB 672 from Madrid to Miami. Read about them below. Then listen to their conversation, and <u>underline</u> the correct information.

Her name is Carmen Morales. She's from Madrid.

She's travelling to Miami *for a holiday/on business.* She has *one child/three children.* She feels *calm/excited/worried.*

She *has been to Miami two or three times before/travels to Miami regularly.*

Her name is Audrey Wilkinson. She's from Glasgow, in Scotland.

It's her *first/second* flight.

She's flying to Miami to see her *grandson/granddaughter. He's/She's two months/two years* old.

She feels *calm/excited/worried.*

**Listening for language**

1  Look at the sentences below and say where you usually hear them and who says them.

**Where**
– at the check-in desk
– on the plane
– at the customs
– at the arrivals gate

**Who**
– the pilot
– the ground staff
– the cabin staff
– the customs officer

– the person meeting you

a. ☒ Smoking or non-smoking?

b. ☐ Please fasten your seat-belts.

c. ☐ Would you like something to drink?

d. ☐ How many bags have you got, please?

e. ☐ Can you open these suitcases, please?

f. ☐ This is Captain Lucas welcoming you aboard Flight IB 672 from Madrid to Miami.

g. ☐ I hope you had a good flight!

h. ☐ Have a good flight!

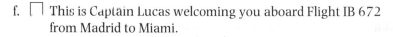

**T.2b**

2  You will now hear the eight sentences in 1 above. Mark them S if they are the same as the ones in 1, and D if they are different. The first one has been done for you.

◀ **T.2b**

3  Listen again and change the words that are different from what you heard.
Example

> comfortable
> Have a ~~good~~ flight!

**Speaking**

Think about a journey you have been on by plane, and which you remember well. (If you have never flown, you can talk about a journey by car/train, etc.)

Work with a partner. Each describe your journey, using these questions to help you:

– Why was the journey important?
– When was the journey?
– Where did you fly from/to?
– How did you get to the airport?
– Who was with you?
– How did you feel before the flight?
– What time did you leave/arrive?
– Was it a comfortable flight?
– Did anything unusual happen?

What other questions can you ask?

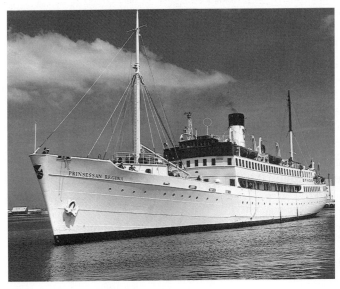

# 3 Everything you need to know

**Before you listen**

**1** What are the names of the places and things below?

**2** When you first arrive in a new town or foreign country, you sometimes need to find the places or things above. Why? Fill the gaps in the phrases below with a verb from the box. (Some verbs can be used more than once.) Then match the phrases with the pictures in 1.

a. to _____ stamps     f. to _____ a train

b. to _____ your family     g. to _____ traveller's cheques

c. to _____ letters     h. to _____ friends

d. to _____ money     i. to _____ a bus

e. to _____ a newspaper     j. to _____ postcards

> buy     change     post     send     phone     catch

**3** If you want to find one of the places or things in 1, what questions do you ask?

**Listening for information**

Ebru is from Turkey. She arrived in London yesterday and is asking Mrs Bell, her landlady, about useful places nearby.

T.3a

**1** Listen to their conversation and answer the questions below.

   a. Which two things/places does Ebru want to find?
   b. Why does she need to find them?

**2** Ebru speaks very good English, but she finds Mrs Bell very difficult to understand. Why, do you think?

◄ T.3a

**3** Listen again. Which of the things below did Mrs Bell say? (It doesn't matter if the words are not exactly the same.) Tick (√) the ones that you hear.

   a. ☐ The nearest post box is in front of the post office.
   b. ☐ At the end of the road you turn left to go up the hill.
   c. ☐ At the top of the hill you turn left.
   d. ☐ The post office is the first shop on your left.
   e. ☐ The station is in the same street as the post office.
   f. ☐ The station is on the other side of the road from the post office.

**Listening for language**

**1** Ebru is very polite during the conversation when she wants to find out information *and* when she doesn't understand Mrs Bell. Here are some of the things she says. Can you put the words in the correct order?

   a.   you   I   can   ask   something   ?

   b.   slowly   say   you   that   more   again   could   ?

   c.   understand   I   last   the   part   didn't   .

   d.   didn't   well   very   I   understand   sorry   .

   e.   you   me   again   tell   could   ?

   f.   something   else   can   ask   I   you   ?

| T.3b | 〜0 | **2** | Listen and check your answers. |

Practice saying the questions and phrases on the tape.

**Speaking**   **1**   Work in pairs. Act out the conversation between A and B in a library. Check the meaning of the words and phrases below before you start.

> a *library*　　　　　to *borrow* a book
> to *join* a library　　a library *fine*
> a *librarian*

**Student A**

You would like to join the library. You want to know the answers to these questions.

> How many books can I borrow?

> What times does the library open and close every day?

> Is there a quiet place where I can study?

> Where can I find Shakespeare's plays?

You ask the librarian, who speaks very quickly and gives a lot of information, like Mrs Bell. Use some of the phrases from the tape to ask questions and to make sure that you understand clearly.

**Student B**

You are the librarian. Like Mrs Bell, you speak very quickly and you give a lot of information. A will ask you some questions. You will find the answers in the answer key on page 70. Practise reading the answers so that you can say them quickly.

**2**   Change roles and act out the conversation again.

# 4 At the bank

**1**    Do you know the names for these in English? Choose from the words below.

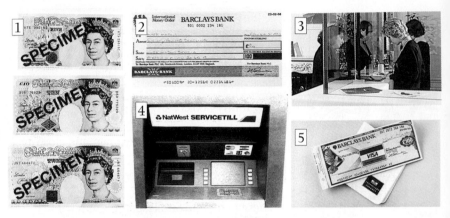

| | |
|---|---|
| bank notes     cash dispenser     cashier     traveller's cheques international money order | |

**2**    Here is some information about banks in Britain. Is the same true for banks in your country? Mark each sentence *same* or *different*.

| | Same | Different |
|---|:---:|:---:|
| – Banks are open from 9.30 in the morning to 4.30 in the afternoon. | ☐ | ☐ |
| – Banks don't close at lunchtime. | ☐ | ☐ |
| – Banks don't usually open on Saturdays. | ☐ | ☐ |
| – Many people get their money from cash dispensers. | ☐ | ☐ |
| – These are open 24 hours. | ☐ | ☐ |
| – It's easy for a foreigner to open a bank account. All you need is a letter of reference. | ☐ | ☐ |

**3** Compare your answers with your partner's. If the information is different in your country, make a sentence.

Example
*Banks are open from 10.00 in the morning to 5.00 in the afternoon.*

**Listening for information**

T.4a

**1** You will hear five dialogues in a bank. Which dialogue goes with which picture?

T.4a

**2** Listen to the dialogues again, and complete the information.

Dialogue 1  The customer wants to change $_____ into pounds sterling.
He receives £_____ .

Dialogue 2  The customer wants to cash a traveller's cheque for £_____ .

Dialogue 3  The customer's name is _____ .

Dialogue 4  What documents does the customer need to open a bank account?

Dialogue 5  How many notes does the cashier give the customer?

2 ☐    3 ☐    4 ☐    7 ☐    20 ☐

| **Listening for language** | **1** | Look at these sentences from the dialogues. In each case, one word is incorrect. <u>Underline</u> the incorrect word in each sentence. The first example has been done for you. |

a. I'd like to change this <u>with</u> pounds sterling, please.
b. I'd like to exchange a traveller's cheque, please.
c. Can you signature here, please?
d. Are the money here?
e. I want opening a bank account here.
f. How do you like the money?
g. Can I to have three twenty pound notes and four tens, please?

**T.4b**    **2**   Listen to the sentences and correct the words that you have underlined.

   **3**   Who said each sentence, the customer or the cashier?

**4**   Practise saying the customer's sentences. Copy the voices on the tape.

| **Speaking** | **1** | Work in pairs, A and B. A is the cashier, B is the customer. Act out the three situations below and opposite. |

**Situation 1**
The customer wants to change some currency into pounds sterling. The amount is equal to £200 and the bank charges a commission of 2%.

Start the conversation like this:

**Situation 2**
The customer wants to change a traveller's cheque for £100 in £10 notes.

Start the conversation like this:

**Situation 3**

The customer is expecting a money order of $500 from home. The cashier needs this customer's name and some identification. Decide if the money order has arrived or not.

Start the conversation like this:

**2** Change roles. B is the cashier and A is the customer.

# 5 Starting conversations

**Before you listen**

Most people enjoy a good conversation, but sometimes it's difficult to know how to start!

Look at the pictures. What do you think the people are talking about? Do they know each other well? What is the relationship between them? Use the words below to help you.

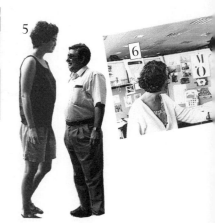

| business associates | classmates | friends | neighbours |
|---|---|---|---|
| colleagues | landlady/lodger | mother and son/daughter | strangers |

**Listening for information**

T.5a

**1** Now listen to the conversations that go with the pictures above. In the first column below, write the relationship between the speakers. In the second column, write what they are talking about. The first one is done for you.

| | Relationship | Conversation about |
|---|---|---|
| 1 | *classmates* | *weekend* |
| 2 | | |
| 3 | | |
| 4 | | |
| 5 | | |
| 6 | | |

◀ T.5a

**2** Listen again, and find the answers to the following questions.

a. Who enjoyed their weekend more, the boy or the girl?

_____

b. What did the woman have to eat or drink on the train?

_____

c. Where are the young couple from exactly?

_____

d. Did the young man like the film? What was its title?

_____

e. What is the woman neighbour going to do this weekend?

_____

f. Where and when did the woman buy her pullover?

_____

**Listening for language**

T.5b

**1** You will hear six questions from the dialogues. Choose the best answer for each question (a., b., or c.).

1 a. Thanks. The same to you.
   b. How about you?
   c. Yes, it was great!

2 a. Yes, fine thanks, ... very comfortable.
   b. Well, just a sandwich and a coffee.
   c. Oh, thank you very much.

3 a. Yes, we like it very much.
   b. We're from a place called Hamilton.
   c. Yes, we're here on holiday.

4 a. It was called *The Lost Dream*.
   b. It was all right.
   c. I think it'll be good.

5 a. Yes. We like the seaside.
   b. Yes. We went to the seaside.
   c. Yes. We're taking the children to the seaside.

6 a. I'm buying a new one on Saturday.
   b. Yes, thanks.
   c. Oh, thanks. Yes, I got it on Saturday.

T.5c

**2** Now listen and practise the questions and answers. Copy the voices on the tape.

**Speaking**

**1** Look at the conversation below. What is the relationship between the speakers? What are they talking about?

**A** Good morning, Mariko. How are you?
**B** I'm fine, thanks.
**A** Did you have a nice weekend?
**B** Very nice thanks. We went on an excursion.
**A** Oh, really? Where did you go?
**B** We went to Bath. It was very interesting. How was *your* weekend?
**A** Oh, nothing special. I was marking compositions most of the time. By the way, did you do your homework?
**B** Oh, er … .

**2** Choose one (or more) of the situations in the pictures. Prepare an eight-line dialogue like the one above. Try to use some of the expressions you have learnt in this unit.

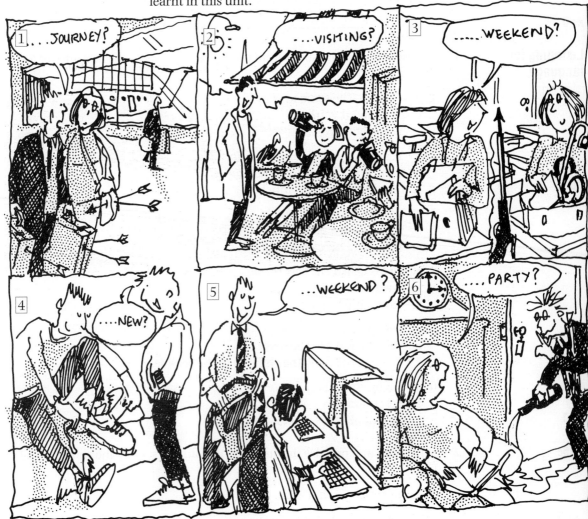

# 6 Looking for somewhere to stay

**1** Work in pairs. When you stay in a hotel in a strange town, which of these things are most important to you? Why?

- It's cheap.
- You can pay by credit card.
- Each room has a private bathroom.
- There's a good restaurant.
- You can get single rooms as well as double rooms.

- It's in a central position in the town.
- There's a bar.
- There's a TV in the bedroom.
- It's modern.
- It's clean.

**2** Robert and Johanna are looking for a hotel. Read about them below, then answer the questions.

*One of the British forms of Mastercard.

Robert and Johanna are on a touring holiday in Switzerland, and have just arrived in a small town. They are looking for a hotel near the centre of town for the next three nights. They hope to find a double room with a private bathroom for under 200 francs. As they don't have much cash they would like to pay by Access*. In the main square of the town they can see three hotels: Hotel Astoria, Hotel Montrose, and Hotel Jungfrau. Johanna goes to ask about rooms in the three hotels while Robert waits in the car.

a. What is most important to Robert and Johanna?

b. How much do they want to pay?

c. How long do they want to stay?

## Listening for information

**T.6a/b/c**

**1** Listen to Johanna's conversations in the three hotels and complete the table below. Write a question mark (?) if the tape does not give the answer. You will need to listen more than once.

| | Hotel Jungfrau | Hotel Montrose | Hotel Astoria |
|---|---|---|---|
| Is there a double room available? | | | |
| Does it have a private bathroom? | | | |
| Can they stay for three nights? | | | |
| How much is it a night? | | | |
| Can they pay by Access? | | | |

**2** Work in pairs. Which hotel do you think Robert and Johanna should stay in? Or do you think they should try to find another one? Act out their conversation.

**Listening for language**

1 Here are different lines from the conversation in the Hotel Astoria. Can you put the lines into the right order?

☐ A double room with a private bathroom is 440 francs a night.

☐ Yes, we take all credit cards.

☐ Right. Thanks. Er, I'll just speak to my husband …

☐ Hello. Can I help you?

☐ Can you tell me the price?

☐ Mm. And do you take Access?

☐ Yes. We've got rooms available. That's fine.

☐ Yes. I'm looking for a double room for the next three nights. Have you got anything?

 ☐──○ 2 Listen to the conversation again and check your answers.

3 Practise the conversation with your partner, using the tapescript on page 60.

4 Practise it again without reading from the book. It doesn't matter if you don't use exactly the same words.

**Speaking**

Robert and Johanna decide to try another hotel, the Grand Victoria. They are now feeling tired and impatient. The receptionist at the hotel is very slow and not very helpful.

Work in pairs. Act out the conversation between the receptionist and Johanna/Robert. (Information for the receptionist is on page 72.)

# 7     **Going sightseeing**

Work with a partner. Discuss the following questions:

– Do you enjoy looking round cities? What kind of places do you enjoy visiting?

– What is the most interesting city that you have visited? Why?

– Which cities would you most like to visit? Why?

– Below are the names of eight places in a famous city. Which city is it? What do you know about these places?

☐ Broadway
☐ Central Park
☐ The Empire State Building
☐ Greenwich Village

☐ Harlem
☐ The Metropolitan Museum of Art
☐ The Statue of Liberty
☐ The World Trade Center

– Have you ever visited New York? Which places did you like best? Did you visit any other interesting places?

*Or*

– Would you like to visit New York? Why/why not?

**Listening for information**

Alex, a young Englishman, is staying in New York with Lindsay and Jack, some friends of his parents. He is only there for two days and wants to see as much as possible. He is talking to Lindsay about the most interesting places to visit.

T.7a

1 Listen to the whole conversation and tick (√) the places opposite that they talk about. Which other places do they mention?

◄ T.7a

2 Read the statements below. Then listen to the conversation again. Stop at the end of each part. Put a tick (√) in the box if the statement is true and a cross (x) if it is false.

Part 1

a. ☐ Alex already knows New York quite well.

b. ☐ Lindsay likes the view from the Empire State Building in the morning.

c. ☐ She thinks Alex should also go to the World Trade Center building to see the view.

Part 2

a. ☐ Alex likes shopping more than art galleries.

b. ☐ Lindsay thinks that Alex should spend two days at the Metropolitan Museum of Art.

c. ☐ Lindsay thinks that it's a bad idea to go to Central Park because it's dangerous.

Part 3

a. ☐ The boats which stop at the Statue of Liberty are more expensive than the ones that don't stop.

b. ☐ Alex wants to do the cheaper boat trip.

c. ☐ Alex decides to visit the museum on Ellis Island.

d. ☐ Lindsay thinks it will be impossible to visit all these places in one day.

**Listening for language**

1 Below are some lines from Alex and Lindsay's conversation. Match a line in **A** with a line in **B**. An example has been done for you.

| A | | B | |
|---|---|---|---|
| 1 ☐ What should I do first? | | a. ☐ Really? How far is it? | |
| 2 ☑ You *have* to do that! | | b. ☐ Sure. I'll go and get it! | |
| 3 ☐ It's a long way, you know! | | c. ☐ Well, there are different ways to do that. You can take a tour … | |
| 4 ☐ Have you got a map, perhaps? | | d. ☐ I think you should start with the Empire State Building. | |
| 5 ☐ I must see the Statue of Liberty! | | e. ☐ Well, it depends what you like. | |
| 6 ☐ What else do you recommend? | | f. ☑ Mm. It sounds great! | |

2 Who said which lines in 1 above? Put A in the box if it was Alex, and L if it was Lindsay. An example has been done for you.

T.7b ☞ 3 Listen to the extracts from the conversations and check your answers.

**Speaking**

1 Work with a partner. Each of you think of a different city that you know (your own city, another city in your country, or a city in another country).

**Student A**
You are a foreign tourist. You have just two or three days to see B's city.

**Student B**
Give advice to A about the best places to visit. Try to find out first what kind of things A is interested in.

2 Before you begin, look at the phrases in **Listening for language** 1 again. Underline and practise saying the ones that will be useful in the conversation. Act out the conversation.

3 Change roles. Again, before you start, underline and practise the phrases that will be useful in the conversation.

# 8 At the travel agent's

**Before you listen**

**1**  Discuss these questions in groups.

– Do you travel very much? Why do you travel, usually?

– Which types of travel have you tried? (plane, boat, hitch-hiking, etc.) Which do you like best? Why?

– When you travel, do you like to book everything a long time in advance? Why/why not?

**2**  Check the meaning and pronunciation of the words below.

| a flight | a return (ticket) | to book | full |
|----------|-------------------|---------|------|
| a deposit | a single (ticket) | the price | an airline |

Which type of travel do they all relate to?

**Listening for information**

Ken is from Hong Kong. He is studying in Britain, but wants to fly home to spend the summer holidays with his family. To find out about flights, he goes to Transworld Travel – a travel agency which specializes in cheap travel for young people.

**1**  Work with a partner. What questions will Ken ask the travel agent, do you think? Write your questions in the box below.

> 1 _____
> 2 _____
> 3 _____
> 4 _____

T.8

**2**  Listen to Ken's conversation with the travel agent and tick (√) the questions in 1 that you heard. (If the idea is the same, it doesn't matter if the words are different.) What are the travel agent's answers to your questions?

◀ T.8

**3** Below are some more questions on the conversation. Cross out (~~cross out~~) the questions that you have already answered. Listen again and answer the other questions.

> 1 How many prices does the travel agent give Ken?
> 2 How much does the cheapest flight cost?
> 3 How much does the most expensive flight cost?
> 4 Which one is Ken interested in?
> 5 Which days of the week does it go?
> 6 How many hours does it take?
> 7 How long does it stop over for?
> 8 Is it better to book now?
> 9 How much deposit will Ken have to pay?
> 10 When will he have to pay the full price?

**Listening for language**

**1** Match a line in **A** with a line in **B**.

| A | B |
|---|---|
| 1 Hi. What exactly do you want to know? | a. The total time is about 22 hours – you're in Rome for about four hours. |
| 2 When do you want to travel? | b. Well, it gets quite full. |
| 3 Does it go every day? | c. No, no. Just a £50 deposit. |
| 4 How many hours does it take? | d. Well, first of all, how much does a flight cost? |
| 5 Do I need to book now, do you think? | e. I want to fly out at the end of June and come back about the middle of September. |
| 6 And do I have to pay the full £506 when I book? | f. Mm … no. It goes on Tuesday, Thursday, and Saturday. |

◀ T.8

**2** Listen to the conversation again and check your answers.

**3** Practise the questions and answers, copying the voices on the tape. Then practise reading them with a partner.

**Speaking**

1    Work with a partner. Student A chooses one of the destinations below. Student B chooses the best flight time, price, and deposit from the possibilities below.

| Destinations | Prices | Flight times | Deposits |
|---|---|---|---|
| Buenos Aires | $2,500 | 1½ hours | $20 |
| Cairo | $1,775 | 2½ hours | $100 |
| Lisbon | $1,555 | 4 hours | $250 |
| London | $1,050 | 5½ hours | |
| Los Angeles | $899 | 8 hours | |
| Prague | $725 | 9 hours | |
| Sydney | $555 | 12 hours | |
| Tokyo | $370 | 15 hours | |
| | $195 | 20 hours | |

Use the information above to act out a conversation in the travel agent's.

2    When you have finished, change roles, so that Student B chooses a destination.

# 9 In the pub

1  Here is an extract about English pubs from a guidebook to Britain. Read it and tick (√) the things that you knew before you read this.

## EIGHT THINGS YOU NEVER KNEW ABOUT ENGLISH PUBS

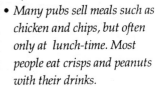

- *Pubs in England cannot open before 11.00 in the morning and have to close at 11.00 in the evening.*
- *Ten minutes before a pub stops serving drinks, the barman shouts 'Last orders'. Many people buy another drink then.*
- *People under 18 years old are not allowed to drink any alcoholic drinks in pubs.*
- *There are no waiters in pubs. The customers go to the bar and order their drinks themselves.*
- *The most common drink is beer, but you can also buy wine, spirits, and soft drinks.*
- *There are several different types of beer - traditional English beer, called 'bitter', is dark brown in colour and not drunk cold. The cold 'yellow' beer drunk in many other countries is called 'lager' in Britain.*
- *When you order a beer in an English pub you ask either for a pint (= a little more than half a litre) or a half (half a pint).*

- *Many pubs sell meals such as chicken and chips, but often only at lunch-time. Most people eat crisps and peanuts with their drinks.*

2  Are these things the same in bars in your country? Have you ever been to a pub in England? Did you have any problems ordering?

3  Look at the photographs opposite. Use the information in the extract above to say what exactly there is in each picture.
Example
*In picture one there's a half of bitter and a packet of crisps.*

## Listening for information

Dieter, a young German, is in London visiting his friend Nick. One day, they arrange to meet in a pub for a drink after Nick has finished work. Nick is a little late, so Dieter decides to buy himself a drink, but he has some problems ordering. When Nick arrives, he explains what happened.

**T.9a**

**1** Listen to Dieter and Nick's conversation and look at the photographs below. Which photograph shows:

a. what Dieter wanted to order?
b. what he got?
c. what he is going to order next?

1

2

3

4

5

6

**T.9a**

**2** Listen to Dieter and Nick's conversation again, reading the tapescript on page 62. With a partner, decide what Dieter and the barman each said in their first conversation. Act out their conversation.

**Listening for language**

1 Dieter goes to order a drink for himself and Nick. Below is his second conversation with the barman, but it is in the wrong order. Can you put it into the correct order?

a. ☐ Can I have a pint of bitter, a half of lager, and two packets of crisps, please?

b. ☐ Plain, or cheese and onion?

c. ☐ That's two pounds forty-four, please.

d. ☐ Yes, please?

e. ☐ A pint of lager, did you say?

f. ☐ And how many packets of crisps?

g. ☐ Er, plain, please.

h. ☐ No, a half, please.

i. ☐ Two, please.

T.9b 🔑 2 Listen and check your answers.

3 Practise reading the dialogue with a partner.

**Speaking**

Work in pairs.

*Either*
You are in an English pub.

**Student A**
You are the customer. You are ordering drinks and crisps for yourself and five friends. You all want something different to drink. Decide what you are going to ask for.

**Student B**
You are the barman. You are not very good at remembering orders. Decide what questions you will ask when you want the customer to repeat him/herself.

*Or*
Nick is visiting you in your country. You are in a café or a bar, and he wants to order a drink and a snack, but he doesn't know what kind of things he can order. You describe to him some typical drinks or snacks. Act out your conversation.

# Friends for dinner

**1** What happens in your country when someone invites you for a meal? Here is a list of things that could happen in Britain. Decide if each one happens *before* you eat, *while* you eat, or *after* you eat. The first one has been done for you.

| Bring flowers/something to drink | *before* |
|---|---|
| Prepare the food | |
| Do the washing up | |
| Say something nice about the food | |
| Offer to help in the kitchen | |
| Lay the table | |
| Thank the hosts | |
| Serve the food | |
| Offer something to drink | |

**2** Who usually does the things in 1, the *hosts* or the *guests*?

Make some sentences using *always*, *usually*, *sometimes*, and *never*.

Example
*(In my country) the guests always bring flowers/the hosts usually lay the table.*

**Listening for information**

Bruce and his Hungarian wife, Anna, live in England.
Fiona and Tom are friends of Bruce and Anna's.

**1** One Saturday evening, Bruce and Anna invite Fiona and Tom to their house for dinner. Look at the six pictures and discuss what happened.

**T.10a**

**2** You will now hear six conversations, one for each picture. With each picture, there is a difference between what you hear on the tape, and what you see in the picture. What are the six differences? The first example has been done for you.

| | In the picture | On the tape |
|---|---|---|
| 1 | Anna is making the salad. | Bruce is making the salad. |
| 2 | | |
| 3 | | |
| 4 | | |
| 5 | | |
| 6 | | |

**Listening for language**

1   Here are some phrases which are useful if you're at home with some English-speaking people. Which ones do the *hosts* say? Which one do the *guests* say? Put G (Guests) or H (Hosts) in each box.

a. ☐ Come in!

_____

b. ☐ Would you like something to drink?

_____

c. ☐ Do you need any help?

_____

d. ☐ Mm. That looks delicious!

_____

e. ☐ That was *lovely!*

_____

f. ☐ Would you like some more?

_____

g. ☐ Thank you for having us.

_____

T.10b

2   Listen to the phrases on the tape. All the phrases need an answer. Write the answers you hear under the phrases in 1.

◀ T.10b

3   Listen again and repeat the phrases and the answers. Practise the dialogues with a partner.

**Speaking**

Work in groups of three (A, B, and C). You have invited two students to cook a meal with you, but you all have different ideas. Use the expressions below and the information in A, B, and C to agree on the arrangements.

Examples
*I think we should ... Let's ... Shall I ...? Shall we ...? I'll ... if you want.*

> **A** You like healthy, light food. You don't eat meat. Wine is not very important to you. You do not want to spend too much money. You love cooking and think that you are a very good cook.
>
> **B** Food is not very important to you – you prefer to spend most of the money on drinks. You hate cooking. You don't want to spend too much money.
>
> **C** You love rich food in creamy sauces, especially meat. You think good wine is very important with a meal. You love cooking and think that you are a very good cook. It is not important to you how much money you spend – you just want to have an excellent meal.

# 11 Hiring a car

**Before you listen**

1    Discuss the following questions with a partner.

- Can you drive?
- Do you like driving? Or would you like to learn?
- Have you ever hired a car? Where and why? Did you have any problems?
- How much does it cost to hire a car in your country?
- Have you ever driven in a foreign country? Was it different from driving in your country? What were the differences?

2    Look at the words below, and mark them like this:

   √    the words that you already know
   ?    the words you think you know
   x    the words you don't know

| | |
|---|---|
| a credit card | insurance (*n*) |
| a driving licence | tax (VAT) (*n*)* |
| identification (*n*) | unlimited mileage** (*n*) |
| | to include |

\*   See
\*\*   answer
    key

Compare your answers with those of two or three other students. Explain any words that you know, but they don't. Are there any words that no one knows? Ask your teacher or check them in a dictionary.

## Listening for information

Carol, Steve, and their French friend, Isabelle, want to go to Scotland for a week's holiday next month. They have decided to hire a car so that they can tour around. Carol has phoned four car hire companies to get information about prices and other things.

**1** Here are the notes Carol made. Some of the information is the same for all the companies. Read her notes and find the differences.

\* Types of small car

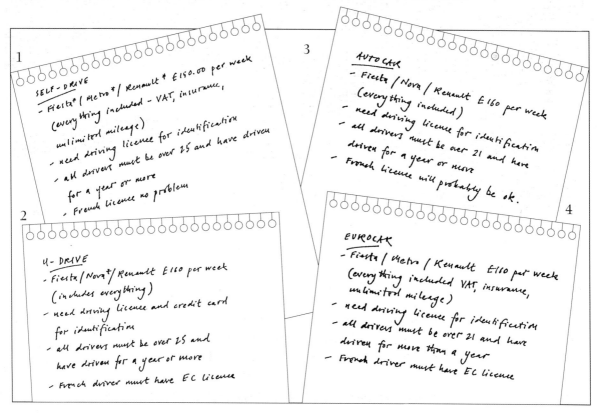

**1**

SELF - DRIVE
- Fiesta\* / Metro\* / Renault \* £150.00 per week
(everything included - VAT, insurance, unlimited mileage)
- need driving licence for identification
- all drivers must be over 25 and have driven for a year or more
- French licence no problem

**2**

U - DRIVE
- Fiesta / Nova\* / Renault £160 per week
(includes everything)
- need driving licence and credit card for identification
- all drivers must be over 25 and have driven for a year or more
- French driver must have EC licence

**3**

AUTO CAR
- Fiesta / Nova / Renault £160 per week
(everything included)
- need driving licence for identification
- all drivers must be over 21 and have driven for a year or more
- French licence will probably be ok.

**4**

EUROCAR
- Fiesta / Metro / Renault £150 per week
(everything included VAT, insurance, unlimited mileage)
- need driving licence for identification
- all drivers must be over 21 and have driven for more than a year
- French driver must have EC licence

T.11a

**2** You will now hear one of Carol's conversations. Listen and decide which set of notes goes with this conversation. Explain why.

**Listening for language**

T.11b

1   During the conversation, Carol asked a lot of questions. You will hear some of these questions again, each one twice. Listen and count the number of words you hear. Write the number in the box on the left.

a. ☐ Can _____ information _____ ?

b. ☐ And _____ include?

c. ☐ What _____ identification _____ ?

d. ☐ And can _____ driver?

e. ☐ Isabelle, _____
    driving licence?

◀ T.11b   ━○    2   Try to fill in the gaps in the questions in 1. Listen and check your answers.

   3   Practise saying the questions. Copy the voices on the tape.

**Speaking**

Work with a partner.

*Either*

Act out Carol's conversation with one of the other car-hire companies, using the notes on page 41 to help you.

*Or*

Imagine that Carol is in your country on holiday. She wants to hire a car and goes to a car-hire company where English is spoken. Act out her conversation. (It doesn't matter if you don't know exactly what the prices for hiring a car are!)

# 12 Going to the gym

**1** How interested in sport are you? Do the following quiz to find out.

## HOW SPORTY ARE YOU?

**❶** Which of these sports and activities have you tried? (✓ = yes, ✗ = no)

- aerobics
- jogging
- swimming
- athletics
- karate
- tennis
- cycling
- mountain climbing
- weight-lifting
- football
- sailing
- yoga
- horse-riding
- skiing

Others ....................................................................

**❷** Write your level next to each of the sports that you have tried.

beg = beginner
int = intermediate
adv = advanced

**❸** Look again at the sports and activities that you did not tick. Which ones would you like to try?

**❹** How often do you do sport or exercise?
- a. every day
- b. 3-5 times a week
- c. 1-2 times a week
- d. 1-2 times a month
- e. never

**❺** Tick (✓) the statements below that you agree with.

- a. Sport is one of the most important things in my life.
- b. I prefer watching sport to doing it.
- c. I don't like watching sport on TV. I prefer doing it myself.
- d. When I was younger I did a lot of sport but I don't do very much now.
- e. I do sport because I think it's a good way to meet people.
- f. I like one or two sports but I find most other sports boring.
- g. If I can, I will continue doing sport until I'm old.
- h. I love exercise because it makes me feel healthy and relaxed.
- i. I don't really like exercise but I do it to lose weight.

### SCORE

**1** Give yourself one point for every sport you have tried.
**2** Give yourself an extra point for every sport at intermediate level; two extra points for every sport at advanced level.
**3** Give yourself a point for every sport that you would like to try.
**4** a. 10  b. 8  c. 6  d. 2  e. 0
**5** a. 5  b. 0  c. 2  d. 1  e. 1
   f. 1  g. 3  h. 3  i. 2

## CONCLUSIONS

**Over 45** - You are sports crazy! You are very fit and probably one of those people who is naturally good at sport. You don't really understand other people who don't like sport. Fine, but make sure that it doesn't become the only thing in your life. It is important to have time for other interests too!

**25-44** - You have a good balance. Sport is important for you. You like to be fit and healthy, and you have a lot of fun doing sport. However, you have many other interests and enjoy being with different types of people.

**10-24** - Not too bad! You know that exercise is important for your health and you try to do something but not often enough. Perhaps you have not yet found the best sport for you. It is much easier to do exercise regularly if you enjoy what you are doing!

**Under 10** - You are not very sporty! Your idea of exercise is getting up to turn on the TV or walking to the fridge for another drink! Perhaps you are unfit and find exercise hard work. Maybe you have not found the best sport for you yet. Why not try something new? Remember to start gently, though.

**2** Compare your score with that of other students in the group. Who got the highest and the lowest score? Are the conclusions true, do you think?

**3** Have you ever been to classes for any of the sports mentioned? Did you enjoy them? Do you prefer doing sports with other people or on your own?

## Listening for information

T.12a

Cathy, a young Canadian, wants to go to an aerobics class at The Fitness Centre, a London gym. She speaks to the receptionist, who gives her the information sheet below. Listen to her conversation and fill in the gaps.

# THE *FITNESS* CENTRE

| NAME OF CLASS | MONDAY – (1) _____ | LEVEL | PRICE (£1 entrance fee ** +) |
|---|---|---|---|
| *Aerobics* | 8.30 - 9.30 | (4) _____ | £2.50 |
| *Aerobics* | (2) _____ | Beg/Int | £2.50 |
| (3) _____ | 5.30 - 6.30 | Beg/Int | £2.50 |
| *Jazz dance* | 6.30 - 7.30 | Beg/Int | (5) _____ |

** (6) *Sauna free in mornings/afternoons/evenings*

## Listening for language

1 Here is part of Cathy's conversation with the receptionist. Can you fill in the gaps?

C Can (a)____ give me (b)____ information about days and times, please?

R Yes, there (c)____ four classes (d)____ day, every day (e)____ Monday (f)____ Saturday - nothing (g)____ Sunday.

C Yeah.

R The first one is (h)____ aerobics class (i)____ 8.30 (j)____ 9.30 (k)____ (l)____ morning. Then there's another aerobics class (m)____ lunch-time from 12.30 to 1.30.

C Right.

R Then (n)____ the evening from 5.30 to 6.30 - that's aerobics too. (o)____ there's a jazz dance class from 6.30 to 7.30.

T.12b

2 Listen and check your answers.

3 Practise reading the dialogue with a partner.

**Speaking**  **1**  Work with a partner and do both activities below.

Activity 1

**Student A**
You go to the Jubilee Sports Centre to get information about the swimming pool. You want to know
– times/days
– prices
– if there's a sauna (and the price)
Make notes about the information that you receive.

**Student B**
You are the receptionist at the Jubilee Sports Centre. Look at the information sheet on page 77 and find the answers to A's questions.

Activity 2

**Student B**
You go to the Jubilee Sports Centre to get information about yoga classes. You want to know
– times/days
– prices
– levels
Make notes about the information that you receive.

**Student A**
You are the receptionist at the Jubilee Sports Centre. Look at the information sheet on page 78 to find the answers to B's questions.

**2**  When you have finished, check the notes you made with the information sheets on pages 77 and 78. Did you understand/give the information correctly?

# 13 At the chemist's

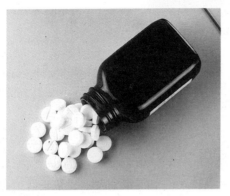

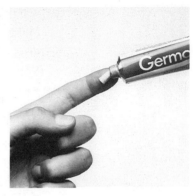

**Before you listen**

1 People sometimes ask advice about medical problems at the chemist's. Look at the three medical problems below. Do you know what they are?

| Headache | Sunburn | Diarrhoea |

All the words in the box below relate to these problems. Write them in the diagram as in the example. Use each word or phrase only once.

| | | | |
|---|---|---|---|
| vomiting | fair skin | burn | sunscreen lotion |
| medicine | see a doctor | paracetamol | cream |
| an aspirin | tablets | a spoonful of medicine | keep it covered up |

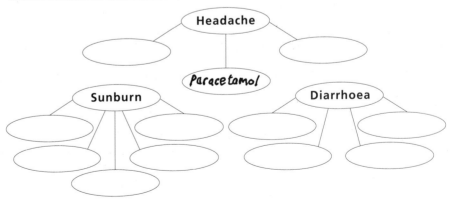

2 Make sure that you can pronounce all the words and phrases correctly.

46

## Listening for information

Mala is a pharmacist. The chemist's where she works is in a popular holiday town. Tourists often come in to buy things and ask her questions.

**T.13a**

1 Listen to three conversations about the problems in **Before you listen**. Check that you have written the words in the box under the correct problem. Number the words (1, 2, 3, etc.) in the order that you hear them in the conversations.

◀ **T.13a**

2 Now listen to each conversation separately. Each time, listen for the answers to these three questions:

a. Who is the medicine for?
b. What does the customer buy at the end of the conversation?
c. Does the pharmacist give any advice?

**Listening for language**

**1** Look at the pairs of questions below. Both a. and b. are possible and correct English, but only *one* of them is from the conversations you have just heard. Listen to the conversations again and <u>underline</u> the one that you heard (a. or b.).

T.13b

1 a. Have you got anything for … ?
  b. Have you got something for … ?

2 a. How many should I take?
  b. How many can I take?

3 a. Do I pay here?
  b. Can I pay here?

4 a. May I have a look at her arms?
  b. Could I have a look at her arms?

5 a. Which cream do you recommend?
  b. Which one do you recommend?

6 a. Who is it for?
  b. Is it for an adult?

7 a. How serious is it?
  b. How bad is it?

**2** Can you remember who asked each question, the pharmacist or the customer? Practise saying the questions that you heard on the tape.

**Speaking**

**1** Choose one of the conversations from the tape and act it out with a partner, using some of the questions and vocabulary from this unit.

**2** Work with your partner again. A is the pharmacist. B is a customer who comes into the chemist's to ask for something to help these people:

 – a child with a cough
 – an adult with flu
 – a teenager with spots

# 14 Lost and found

**1** Think about the following questions.
  – Have you ever lost anything important?
  – What was it?
  – Where/when did you lose it?
  – What did you do to find it? Did you find it again?

Tell your partner about it.

**2** Debby, an American tourist visiting England with her husband Don, lost her handbag one day. Use the pictures and the phrases below to tell the story of what happened. The phrases are already in the correct order.

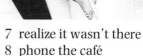

| | |
|---|---|
| 1 be on holiday | 7 realize it wasn't there |
| 2 have a coffee | 8 phone the café |
| 3 walk along the street | 9 apologize |
| 4 put down | 10 go to the police station |
| 5 not notice | 11 describe the bag |
| 6 pick it up | 12 fill in a form |

## Listening for information

**T.14a** 🔑

**1** Listen to Debby and Don's conversation when Debby realizes that she has lost her bag. Then answer the questions below.

a. What does Debby say was in her handbag? Tick (√) the items.

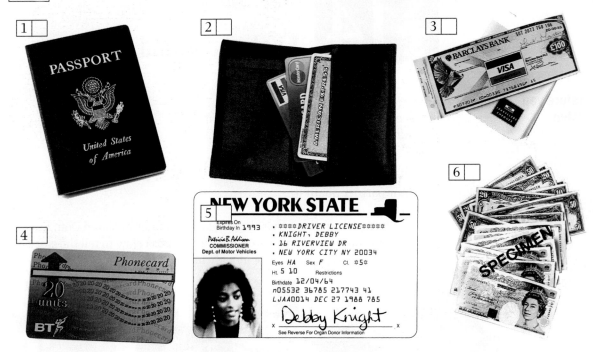

b. Where does Debby think she left the bag?
c. What do they decide to do?

**T.14b** 🔑

**2** Debby spoke to the manageress of the café, who made some notes. Listen to their conversation, and complete the missing information.

**Listening for language**

1 Finally, Debby and Don went to a police station to report the loss of the handbag.

Here are six questions the police officer asked Debby. Choose the correct verb form to complete each question.

1 Where did you last *had/have* it?
2 What *was/were* in it?
3 *Was/were* there any money in it?
4 What *did/was* it look like?
5 What kind of handbag *has it been/was it*?
6 Where did you *leave/left* it exactly?

2 Now match each question with the correct answer.

The first one has been done for you.

a.
**A** On the table, I think.
Q ☐

b.
**A** No, I don't think so.
Q ☐

c.
**A** It was a leather one.
Q ☐

d.
**A** It's light brown – quite a small handbag.
Q ☐

e.
**A** My passport and – oh, everything!
Q ☐

f.
**A** I had it when we were in the café.
Q 1

T.14c  3 Listen and check your answers.

**Speaking**

Work with a partner. One of you has lost a briefcase/handbag.

---

**Student A**

You have come to the police station to report the loss of your briefcase/handbag.

The police officer will ask you:

– your name
– your address/telephone number in England
– where you lost it
– when you lost it
– for a short description and what was in it.

Check you know the answers to these questions before you start.

---

**Student B**

You are a police officer. You must fill in a lost property form like the one below.

Decide what questions you are going to ask before you start. Then complete the lost property form.

---

## LOST PROPERTY FORM

Date: ........../........../..........  Duty officer: ................................................

Name of person reporting loss: .......................................................

Address: .................................................................................................

...............................................................................................................

Lost article: ............................................................................................

Description of lost article: ....................................................................

Contents: ................................................................................................

...............................................................................................................

Place/Time of loss: ................................................................................

Other information: .................................................................................

................................................................ Signed: ..................................

---

Begin your conversation like this:

**Student B** (police officer)  *Yes, sir/madam. Can I help you?*
**Student A**  *Yes, I've lost my briefcase/handbag.*
**Student B**  *I see. Well, I'd better take some details. What is your name, please?*

# 15 Choosing an English course

1   Are you studying English alone, with a private teacher, at school, or at a language school?

If you're studying at a language school, why did you choose this one? Make a list of things you think are important in a language school, like this:

– Friendly teachers
– Easy to get to

Compare your list with your partner's. Which things do you think are *most* important?

2   Read about Marisol, from Spain.

> Hi! My name's Marisol. I'm from Spain – from Madrid. At the moment, I'm living in Hampstead, a suburb of London. I need to improve my English, so I came here to work as an *au pair*. I'm staying with an English couple – Mr and Mrs Burns. In the daytime I clean the house and look after their two children. Now I need to find a good school where I can study for the First Certificate exam. There are so many schools, but it's hard to choose the right one!

**3**   Look at these advertisements for four schools. Which school

- ☐1☐ offers courses for just a few hours a week?
- ☐ tells you the dates when courses begin?
- ☐ tells you how many students there are in a class?
- ☐ *doesn't* mention exam classes?
- ☐ gives the price of courses?
- ☐ tells you what time the classes start/finish?

### St Patrick's College

*London: Regent's Park, Highgate, Folkestone, Bournemouth*

Full and part-time Exam classes and intensive English language courses

Social programmes and excursions
For further information ring
071 386 4167

1

2

ENGLISH IN SMALL CLASSES

### Knightsbridge School of English

33 Brompton Road, London
Tel 071 - 467 3214

*Full-time courses at all levels throughout the year, morning and afternoon.*
*Courses begin:*
*7 January, 4 February, 4 March, 1 April*
*5 to 9 students in a class*
*One-to-one tuition*

### Welcome to LIVING LANGUAGES

West Clapham Common, London SW4

**French • Spanish • German • Japanese**

English for foreign students:

•

Mornings 9-12 and afternoons 2-4

•

Intensive & Examination Courses

•

36 or 28 lessons

•

Friendly atmosphere

3

**OPEN ALL YEAR**

*Fees: £148 for 4 weeks*
*£370 for 12 weeks*
*15 hours per week*

**Learn English at the**

**ENGLISH STUDIES CENTRE**

*66, Park Road, Kensington*
*London W8*
*071 765 8636*
*Fax: 071 765 5203*

**All levels from beginners to advanced Cambridge University & ARELS Oral Exams**

4

**Listening for information**

T.15a

1   Listen to Marisol talking about the four schools with her landlady, Mrs Burns.

Tick (√) the schools which Marisol decides to telephone.

| English Studies Centre | | Knightsbridge School of English | | Living Languages | | St Patrick's College | |
|---|---|---|---|---|---|---|---|
| | | | | | | | |

2   What was the problem with the two schools she decided *not* to telephone?

T.15b

3   Listen to Marisol telephoning St Patrick's College, and complete her notes below.

First Cert?
Times:
Days of part-time course:
Fees:

No. of weeks:
No. of students per class:

**Listening for language**

1   Here are some of the receptionist's answers. Use the prompts below to work out Marisol's questions.

a.  Do/have/courses/Cambridge First Certificate?

Yes, we do. We have special courses for First Certificate and Proficiency.

b.  What time/can/come/class?

Well, there are full-time courses in the morning. That's every day from 9 to 12.

c.  Could/tell/price?

Yes, our fees are £480 for the intensive courses, and £80 for the part-time courses.

d.  How long/course/last?

The full-time course lasts ten weeks, and the part-time course is eighteen.

e.  How many/students/class?

The maximum is twelve.

T.15c

2   Listen and check your answers. With a partner, practise saying the questions and answers.

**Speaking**

Work with a partner.

*Either*

Marisol decides to telephone the English Study Centre too. Act out the conversation between her and the receptionist, using some of the questions from **Listening for language** 1.

*Or*

**Student A**
You are in London to study English. You are staying in the centre of London, so all the schools are convenient for you. Decide which one to phone first and act out the conversation with student B.

**Student B**
You are the receptionist at the school. It is a very bad school and you hate your job. You can invent information about the prices and the classes.

# Tapescript section

## Unit 1

### Tapescript 1a

**Marc** Excuse-moi, tu sais à quelle heure on arrive à Paris?

**Maree** Er, sorry. I don't . . .

**Marc** Ah, do you speak English? Er . . . What time do we arrive in Paris? Do you know?

**Maree** I think about two o'clock. I've got a timetable here. I'll just have a look.

**Marc** Thank you.

**Maree** Yes, we arrive in Paris at 14.05. That's five past two, isn't it?

**Marc** Yes. Thank you very much.
Where are you from – England?

**Maree** No, actually. I'm from Australia.

**Marc** Really? Which city?

**Maree** Well, I'm from Melbourne.

**Marc** Oh. My brother's studying in Sydney.

**Maree** Really?

**Marc** Yes. Are you staying in Paris?

**Maree** Just for two or three days – to see the art galleries . . . and the Eiffel Tower! What about you? Are you from Paris?

**Marc** No, no, I'm not French. I'm from Bruxelles – Brussels, you say.

**Maree** Oh, right. That's Belgium, isn't it?

**Marc** That's right. I have to change trains in Paris.

**Maree** I see. So you're just passing through?

**Marc** More or less. I'm staying with some friends in Paris tonight, then I'm travelling home tomorrow morning to see my family.

**Maree** I see, yeah.

### Tapescript 1b

**Maree** You speak really good English. Did you learn English at school?

**Marc** Yes, and I'm studying English at university, actually. That's why I was in London. I was on an intensive English language course.

**Maree** Oh, really? Great!

**Marc** Yes, it was very good. And you . . . What do *you* do?

**Maree** I'm a teacher. I teach small children in a primary school.

**Marc** Oh, that must be nice!

**Maree** Mm. Sometimes! That's why I can't stay long in Paris. My term starts next week. I'm flying back to Melbourne on Friday.

**Marc** Oh, that's a pity. Are you flying back from Paris?

**Maree** No, from London. It's cheaper if you fly from London.

**Marc** I see. I'm sorry. I haven't introduced myself. My name's Marc.

**Maree** Nice to meet you, Marc. I'm Maree.

**Marc** Marie, as in French?

**Maree** Well, er, yeah . . .

**Marc** Marie, I was just going to the buffet. Would you like to come and have some breakfast?

**Maree** Breakfast? Oh, yeah, that would be nice.

**Marc** OK. I can tell you something about Paris. Which places do you want to . . .?

## Unit 2

### Tapescript 2a

**MW:** Mrs Wilkinson  **C:** Carmen

**MW** Oh, dear. This seat-belt, I can't . . .

**C** Can I help you?

**MW** Oh, thank you. It's this seat-belt . . .

**C** It's very easy – like this . . .
Is this your first flight?

**MW** Oh, no. No, no. I flew from Glasgow to London once, but it was a long time ago.

**C** I see. Are you staying in Miami?

**MW** Yes. I'm going to see my little grandson.

**C** Oh, that's nice.

**MW** Yes, my daughter lives in the United States, so I don't see her very often. She married an American, you see.

**C** That's nice. And how old is your grandson?

**MW** He's two months old. I'm so excited!

**C** I'm sure. I love children – I have a son myself. He's three.

**MW** How lovely! And do you live in Miami?

C No, I live in Madrid, but I go to Miami two or three times a year on business.

MW Oh, dear! What's that noise?

C Don't worry. We're going to take off.

MW Oh, dear!

### Tapescript 2b

**a.** Smoking or non-smoking?

**b.** Please fasten your seat-belts.

**c.** Would you like a drink?

**d.** How many bags, please?

**e.** Can you open this suitcase, please?

**f.** This is Captain Lucas welcoming you aboard flight IB 672 from Madrid to Miami.

**g.** Did you have a good flight?

**h.** Have a comfortable flight!

# Unit 3

### Tapescript 3a

**E:** Ebru    **MB:** Mrs Bell

E Mrs Bell, can I ask you something?

MB Yes, dear, of course. What do you want to know?

E I want to send these postcards to Turkey. I've got the stamps but I don't know where to post them. Is there a post box near here?

MB Now which is the nearest post box? Yes, I think the nearest is the one in front of the post office actually. Yes, definitely. You go out of the house to the end of the road, then you turn right up to the top of the hill. At the top of the hill you turn left, and the post office is about the third shop on the left. The post box is just outside.

E Sorry. I didn't understand very well. Could you say that again more slowly?

MB Yes. Out of the house to the end of the road.

E Yes.

MB Turn right up the hill, and at the top of the hill you turn left and the post office is about the third shop on the left. The post box is outside.

E Sorry, but I didn't understand the last part. Could you tell me again? At the top of the hill what do I do?

MB Sorry, dear, yes. You turn left and I think the post office is the third shop on the left of the street.

E And the post box is outside?

MB That's right.

E Right, thank you. Can I ask you something else?

MB Anything, dear. What is it?

E Well, tomorrow I have to catch the train very early, so I want to find the station today . . .

MB Good idea. That's very easy from the post office. It's in the same street, but on the other side, just a little bit after the post office.

E Oh, great. Thank you very much, Mrs Bell.

MB A pleasure, dear.

### Tapescript 3b

**a.** Can I ask you something?

**b.** Could you say that again more slowly?

**c.** I didn't understand the last part.

**d.** Sorry – I didn't understand very well.

**e.** Could you tell me again?

**f.** Can I ask you something else?

# Unit 4

### Tapescript 4a

**CASH:** Cashier    **CUS:** Customer

**1**

CASH Yes, please?

CUS Hi. I'd like to change this into pounds sterling, please. It's $250.

CASH Right. Thank you.
That's £140. There's a £2.00 commission.

CUS OK. Thank you very much.

**2**

CASH Hello.

CUS Hello. I'd like to cash a traveller's cheque, please.

CASH Right. How much is it for?

CUS One hundred pounds.

CASH Right. Can you sign here, please? Do you have your passport?

CUS Yes. Just a moment . . .

**3**

CASH Yes, can I help you?

CUS Yes. Er . . . I'm waiting for an international money order from Brazil. My parents sent it here two days ago. Is the money here?

CASH Right. Can I have the name, please?

CUS Yes. It's De Oliveira.

CASH Sorry, De Olly . . .?

CUS It's D-E, new word O-L-I-V-E-I-R-A.

CASH Thank you.

**4**

CUS Hello. I'm from Germany, and I'm staying in England for a year. I want to open an account here. What documents do I need, please?

**CASH** Right. We need to see your passport and a letter from your employer, or your place of study if you're a student.

**CUS** Right. That's all?

**CASH** That's all, yes.

**CUS** OK. Thank you.

**5**

**CASH** How would you like the cash?

**CUS** Er . . . sorry?

**CASH** How would you like the money? Would you like tens? Twenties?

**CUS** Oh, I see. Er . . . Can I have three twenty pound notes and four tens, please?

**CASH** Right.

### Tapescript 4b

**a.** I'd like to change this into pounds sterling, please.

**b.** I'd like to cash a traveller's cheque, please.

**c.** Can you sign here, please?

**d.** Is the money here?

**e.** I want to open a bank account here.

**f.** How would you like the money?

**g.** Can I have three twenty pound notes and four tens, please?

# Unit 5

### Tapescript 5a

**1**

**B:** Teenage schoolgirl  **A:** Teenage schoolboy

**A** Nice weekend?

**B** Yes, it was great!

**A** Oh, yes? Did you do anything special?

**B** Yeah, my boyfriend and I went to a barbecue.

**A** Oh, yes?

**B** On Saturday, yeah. It was lovely! How about you?

**A** Oh, nothing special. Just sat at home, really, watched TV . . .

**2**

**F:** Frances Young  **C:** Celia Brown

**F** Celia Brown?

**C** Yes, that's me.

**F** Ah, hello. I'm Frances Young. Nice to meet you.

**C** Hello.

**F** Did you have a good journey?

**C** Yes, fine thanks – very comfortable.

**F** Did you get something to eat on the train?

**C** Yes. Well, just a sandwich and a coffee.

**F** Oh, well, I'm sure you're hungry. Perhaps we should go to the office first, and then have some lunch.

**3**

**TD:** Taxi-driver  **A:** Young man  **B:** Young woman

**TD** Are you just visiting?

**A** Yes, we're here on holiday. Just for two weeks.

**TD** Oh, very nice. And where are you from? Americans, are you?

**B** Canadians, actually.

**TD** Canadians! So where are you from in Canada, then?

**B** We're from a place called Hamilton.

**TD** Where?

**B** Hamilton. It's in the south of Canada, near Toronto . . .

**TD** Oh, I see.

**4**

**M:** Mother  **S:** Son

**M** Hello, Michael. How was the film?

**S** Oh, hi, mum. It was all right.

**M** What did you go and see in the end?

**S** Oh, something called . . . er . . . *The Lost Dream*, I think it was.

**M** Oh, yes? And who was in it?

**S** Um, what's his name . . . er . . . Kevin Gibson.

**M** Oh, I like him. So what was it about then?

**5**

**A:** Woman  **B:** Man

**A** Morning!

**B** Morning! Lovely day, isn't it?

**A** Mm, marvellous.

**B** Are you doing anything special this weekend?

**A** Yes. We're taking the children to the seaside. It's such lovely weather!

**B** Good idea, make the most of it.

**A** Yes. How about you? Any plans?

**B** Well, I think I'll just do some gardening.

**A** Ah, that's nice.

**B** Yes. Just relax, you know.

**6**

**A:** Woman  **B:** Woman

**A** Oh, I like your pullover. Is that new?

**B** Oh, thanks. Yes, I got it on Saturday.

**A** Oh. I really like the colour. It looks good on you.

**B** Thank you. *I* like it.

**A** Where did you get it?

**B** That shop called 'Zed'.

**A** Oh, yes, I know it. It's lovely.

## Tapescript 5b

1   **A**   Nice weekend?
2   **F**   Did you have a good journey?
3   **TD**   Are you just visiting?
4   **M**   How was the film?
5   **B**   Are you doing anything special this weekend?
6   **A**   I like your pullover. Is that new?

## Tapescript 5c

1   **A** Nice weekend?
    **B** Yes, it was great!

2   **F** Did you have a good journey?
    **C** Yes, fine thanks – very comfortable.

3   **TD** Are you just visiting?
    **A** Yes, we're here on holiday.

4   **M** How was the film?
    **S** It was all right.

5   **B** Are you doing anything special this weekend?
    **A** Yes. We're taking the children to the seaside.

6   **A** Oh, I like your pullover. Is that new?
    **B** Oh, thanks. Yes, I got it on Saturday.

# Unit 6

## Tapescript 6a

**J:** Johanna     **R:** Receptionist

**J** Hello. Do you speak English?
**R** Of course. Can I help you?
**J** Yes, I'm looking for a double room for the next three nights. Have you got one available?
**R** That's tonight, Wednesday, and Thursday. Just a moment please.
  Yes, that's fine.
**J** And that's with a bathroom, is it?
**R** All our rooms have private bathrooms, madam.
**J** And how much is it per night?
**R** 230 francs per night, madam.
**J** Mm, I see. Just one more question – You take Access, don't you?
**R** No, I'm sorry. Only American Express and Visa, not Access.
**J** Oh, right . . . Mm. We're looking for somewhere that takes Access, really. Well, thanks anyway.

## Tapescript 6b

**J** Hello.

**R** Good morning. Can I help you?
**J** Oh, good, you speak English.
**R** Yes.
**J** I'm looking for a double room for the next three nights – with a bathroom.
**R** That's until Thursday?
**J** Yes, have you got anything?
**R** Mm. We've got a double room for tonight and tomorrow night, but not for Thursday night.
**J** Oh, dear. *Nothing* for Thursday night?
**R** No, sorry.
**J** Mm. And what about the price?
**R** 150 francs a night. That's for a double room without bathroom. We're very full. We haven't got any more rooms with private bathrooms.
**J** Oh . . . No bathroom . . . Well, thanks anyway.

## Tapescript 6c

**R** Hello. Can I help you?
**J** Yes. I'm looking for a double room for the next three nights. Have you got anything?
**R** Yes . . . we've got rooms available. That's fine.
**J** Er. Can you tell me the price?
**R** A double room with a private bathroom is 440 francs a night.
**J** Mm. And do you take Access?
**R** Yes, we take all credit cards.
**J** Right. Thanks. Er, I'll just speak to my husband.

# Unit 7

## Tapescript 7a

**L:** Lindsay     **A:** Alex

**Part 1**
**L** So what are you going to do while you're here?
**A** Well, I don't know that much about New York really, you know, just the Empire State Building and the Statue of Liberty. You tell me!
**L** You've just got two days, right? You're going to be pretty busy if you want to see all the sights!
**A** I'm planning to start early tomorrow morning. What should I do first?
**L** I think you should start with the Empire State Building. It's not the highest building now, but the view's just beautiful in the morning, when it's clear and fresh. You have to do that!
**A** Mm. It sounds great! I'll definitely do that. Tell me, which is the highest building now?
**L** The World Trade Center building. But you should go there

at night for the view – there's a bar up there and you can relax and look at the lights of the city. It's wonderful!

**A** Right!

## Part 2

**A** What else do you recommend?

**L** Well, it depends what you like – art, shopping, theatre?

**A** Well, not shopping particularly, but yeah, I'd like to see an art gallery or two.

**L** Oh, then you must go to the Met – the Metropolitan Museum of Art, which is just enormous. You could spend two days there! That's by Central Park, so you can take a walk through Central Park at the same time, but not after dark, remember. It's dangerous then.

**A** Right.

**L** And if you like art galleries, there's the Guggenheim, the Museum of Modern Art, . . .

## Part 3

**A** What about the Statue of Liberty? I must see the Statue of Liberty!

**L** Well, there are different ways to do that. You can take a tour. That stops so you can get out and climb up to the top.

**A** Yeah?

**L** Or the cheap way is just to take the regular Statten Island ferry – that's not a tourist boat, so it doesn't stop – but it passes right by.

**A** No, I think I'll be a tourist and climb up to the top!

**L** All right. Well, there's another interesting trip in the same area – to Ellis Island. There's a big museum all about the immigrants who arrived there. That's pretty interesting!

**A** Mm. Yes, I'd definitely like to do that, too.

**L** Sure, but you're going to be pretty busy. You won't be able to do that on the same day as the Met. It's a long way, you know!

**A** Really? How far is it?

**L** Five or six miles at least!

**A** Is it! I've got *no* idea where these places are. Have you got a map, perhaps?

**L** Sure. I'll go and get it, and you can plan your route.

## Tapescript 7b

**1**

**A** I'm planning to start early tomorrow morning. What should I do first?

**L** I think you should start with the Empire State Building.

**2**

**L** The view's beautiful in the morning, when it's clear and fresh. You have to do that!

**A** Mm. It sounds great!

**3**

**A** What else do you recommend?

**L** Well, it depends what you like – art, shopping, theatre?

**4**

**A** What about the Statue of Liberty? I must see the Statue of Liberty!

**L** Well, there are different ways to do that. You can take a tour.

**5**

**L** You won't be able to do that on the same day as the Met. It's a long way, you know!

**A** Really? How far is it?

**6**

**A** I've got *no* idea where these places are. Have you got a map, perhaps?

**L** Sure. I'll just go and get it, and you can plan your route.

# Unit 8

## Tapescript 8

**TA:** Travel agent    **K:** Ken    **E:** Elaine

**TA** Hello. What can I do for you?

**K** Yes. I want to travel back to Hong Kong for the summer holidays, and I just want an idea of prices and things.

**TA** Just a minute. Elaine! There's a gentleman here wants information about Hong Kong. Can *you* help him?

**E** Hi. What exactly do you want to know?

**K** Hi. Well, first of all, how much does a flight cost?

**E** Our cheapest flight is with Alitalia, stopping over in Rome. That's £506.

**K** Return?

**E** Yes, that's return. It's a good price, isn't it?

**K** Very good! What about the other airlines?

**E** With the other airlines, it depends on the time of year. When do you want to travel?

**K** I want to fly out at the end of June and come back about the middle of September.

**E** Mm. That's quite an expensive time of year, but if you wait a moment, I'll give you some other prices, just to give you an idea.

**K** Thanks.

**E** Well, there's Cathay Pacific at £806. That's direct to Hong Kong; or Gulf Air. That's £599, stopping in Dubai; or . . .

**K** The first one – the one for £506. Does it go every day?

**E** Mm . . . no. It goes on Tuesday, Thursday, and Saturday.

**K** How many hours does it take?

**E** The total time is about 22 hours – you're in Rome for about four hours.

**K** Right. Well that one sounds very good. Do I need to book now, do you think?

**E** Well, it gets quite full. If you're sure you're going to travel, it's best to book soon.

**K** And do I have to pay the full £506 when I book?

**E** No, no. Just a £50 deposit. And then you pay the rest six weeks before travelling.

**K** Right. Well, thank you very much. I think that's everything. I'll probably be back to book later this week.

**E** OK, fine.

# Unit 9

### Tapescript 9a

**N:** Nick **D:** Dieter

**N** Hi, Dieter. OK?

**D** Oh, hi, Nick. Yes, I'm fine, except that I had a big problem ordering my drink. I didn't think my English was so bad!

**N** Your English is very good! What kind of problem?

**D** Well, look at this beer I've got here – this warm, brown, English beer – it wasn't what I wanted!

**N** Why, what did you ask for?

**D** Well, I just asked for a small beer. Then the barman asked what type of beer and said lots of names that I didn't understand – and something about a pie or a pine. I didn't understand anything!

**N** Oh, no! He probably said a *pint*! In English you don't ask for a big or a small beer. You ask for either a pint or a half. A pint's the big one.

**D** So this one I've got here is a half?

**N** Yes, that's a half of bitter. Bitter's the name for that type of beer.

**D** Ah, that's what he said – bitter! Well, it's very different from the beer we drink in Germany, I must say.

**N** Yes, I know. *We* call the German type of beer *lager*. So you have to ask for a half of lager, or a pint of lager.

**D** OK. I understand that now. My other problem was chips. I asked for a packet of chips, and the barman said something strange – that they don't have chips in the evening, only at lunch-time. What did he mean?

**N** Yes, they have fish and chips, but I think you meant *crisps*. In England, chips are fried potatoes, you know, French fries. The ones you buy in a packet are crisps.

**D** Well, in the end I didn't get anything to eat. So you see, I did everything wrong!

**N** Well, never mind. You can practise now by buying me a drink – a pint of bitter, please.

**D** You mean you *choose* to drink this warm horrible stuff? So I ask for a pint of bitter, a half of lager, and a packet of crisps. Is that all right?

**N** Absolutely perfect, but ask for *two* packets of crisps. I'm hungry. Good luck!

**D** Thank you.

### Tapescript 9b

**B:** Barman **D:** Dieter

**B** Yes, please?

**D** Can I have a pint of bitter, a half of lager, and two packets of crisps, please?

**B** A pint of lager, did you say?

**D** No, a half, please.

**B** And how many packets of crisps?

**D** Two, please.

**B** Plain, or cheese and onion?

**D** Er, plain, please.

**B** That's two pounds forty-four, please.

# Unit 10

### Tapescript 10a

**1**

**A:** Anna **B:** Bruce

**A** Bruce?

**B** Mm?

**A** Can you come and help me, please?

**B** Mm . . . coming.

**A** Can you start making the salad, please? It's nearly eight o'clock. They'll be here soon!

**B** Yeah. Um . . . What do you want me to do?

**A** Well, here are the tomatoes and the lettuce. Just start cutting it up!

**B** OK, OK.

**B** Ah, they're here. I'll go and let them in.

**A** But Bruce! What about the salad?

**2**

**F:** Fiona **B:** Bruce **T:** Tom **A:** Anna

**F** Hello.

**T** Hi!

**B** Hello. Well, come in!

**T** Thanks. Sorry we're a bit late. You said 7.30, didn't you?

**B** Er . . . did I? Oh, yes.

**T** Anyway, I brought some wine. Here you are, Bruce.

**B** Oh, thank you.

**F** Where's Anna?

**A** I'm coming! I'm just making the salad!

**B** Let me take your coats.

**F** Oh, thanks.

**A** Hi!

**T** Hi, Anna.

**F** How are you? These are for you, Anna.

**A** Oh, flowers! How lovely! Thank you so much. Would you like to come and sit down?

**3**

**B** Would you like something to drink?

**F** Yes, please. Can I have a glass of wine?

**B** Er, yes, sure. Red or white?

**F** White, please.

**B** OK, a glass of white wine. And for you, Tom?

**T** I'll have a mineral water, please.

**B** Right. Um . . . Anna, have we got any mineral water?

**A** Yes, I think so.

**F** Anna, do you need any help?

**A** No, it's OK, thanks.

**4**

**A** Well, here it is.

**F** Mm. That looks delicious!

**A** I hope it is! It's something Hungarian. We call it 'paprikas csirke'. (/pɑːprɪkɑːs tʃiːrke/)

**T** And what's that exactly?

**A** It's chicken with paprika and cream. I hope you like it.

**5**

**A** Fiona, would you like some more?

**F** No, thanks, really. I couldn't. That was *lovely*!

**A** Oh, thank you. Tom? A little more for you?

**T** Well, just a little, thanks.

**6**

**T** Yes . . . Fiona, what time is it?

**F** Oh! It's quarter past twelve!

**T** Oh, it's late. We must go.

**F** Yes, well. Thank you for having us. It was lovely.

**A** Thank you for coming.

**B** Yes, it was nice to see you again.

### Tapescript 10b

**B:** Bruce  **T:** Tom  **F:** Fiona  **A:** Anna

**a. B** Come in!
   **T** Thanks.

**b. B** Would you like something to drink?
   **F** Yes, please. Can I have a glass of wine?

**c. F** Do you need any help?
   **A** No, it's OK, thanks.

**d. F** Mm. That looks delicious!

**A** I hope it is! It's something Hungarian.

**e. F** That was *lovely*!
   **A** Oh, thank you.

**f. A** Would you like some more?
   **F** No, thanks, really.
   **T** Well, just a little, thanks.

**g. F** Thank you for having us.
   **A** Thank you for coming.

# Unit 11

### Tapescript 11a

**M:** Man  **W:** Woman  **I:** Isabelle

**M** Car Hire Service. Can I help you?

**W** Er, yes. I want to hire a car for a week next month. Can you give me some information about prices? I want something fairly cheap.

**M** Well, for a Mercedes . . . Sorry, are you still there?

**W** Yes?

**M** No, seriously . . . The cheapest thing we have is a Fiesta, a Nova, or a Renault and they're £160 a week.

**W** And what does that include?

**M** Everything – insurance, VAT, unlimited mileage . . .

**W** I see. And tell me . . . What kind of identification do I need? Just a driving licence?

**M** That's right.

**W** And can we have more than one driver?

**M** Sure, if they're all over 21 and they've all had a licence for over a year.

**W** Yes, I think so. But, erm, one of them's French. Does that matter?

**M** Has the person got an EC driving licence?

**W** Just a second. Isabelle, have you got an EC driving licence?

**I** No, why?

**W** Nothing. No, she hasn't, I'm afraid.

**M** Okay. Well, I don't think it'll be a problem. I'll have to ask my manager. Just tell her to bring her ordinary licence with her when you come into the office.

**W** Fine, we'll do that. Thanks very much.

**M** You're welcome. Bye.

**W** Bye.

### Tapescript 11b

**a.** Can you give me some information about prices?

**b.** And what does that include?

**c.** What kind of identification do I need?

**d.** And can we have more than one driver?

**e.** Isabelle, have you got an EC driving licence?

# Unit 12

## Tapescript 12a

**R:** Receptionist   **C:** Cathy

**R** Hello?

**C** Er ... a friend told me that you have exercise and dance classes here.

**R** That's right.

**C** Er ... Can you give me some information about days and times, please?

**R** Yes, there are four classes a day, every day from Monday to Saturday – nothing on Sunday.

**C** Yeah.

**R** The first one is an aerobics class from 8.30 to 9.30 in the morning. Then there's another aerobics class at lunchtime from 12.30 to 1.30.

**C** Right.

**R** Then in the evening from 5.30 to 6.30 – that's aerobics too. And there's a jazz dance class from 6.30 to 7.30.

**C** Right. And what level are they for? I mean would they be OK for a beginner?

**R** The morning aerobics – 8.30 to 9.30 – is advanced. All the others are kind of beginner to intermediate level. But let me give you an information sheet.

**C** Thanks. And how much does it cost for a class?

**R** You pay £1 entrance fee to come into the centre and then the classes are £2.50 each and £3.50 for jazz dance. It's there on the sheet.

**C** Oh, yes, I see.

**R** If you become a member, entrance is free and ...

**C** No, it's OK. I'm only in London for two weeks.

**R** Oh, right. That's no good then.

**C** And I guess you have showers and everything?

**R** Yes, sure, and in the evenings you can use the sauna free, too.

**C** Oh, great. Right. So the next class is at 5.30? Well, I'll see you then.

**R** Fine. See you later!

## Tapescript 12b

**C** Can you give me some information about days and times, please?

**R** Yes, there are four classes a day, every day from Monday to Saturday – nothing on Sunday.

**C** Yeah.

**R** The first one is an aerobics class from 8.30 to 9.30 in the morning. Then there's another aerobics class at lunchtime from 12.30 to 1.30.

**C** Right.

**R** Then in the evening from 5.30 to 6.30 – that's aerobics too. And there's a jazz dance class from 6.30 to 7.30.

# Unit 13

## Tapescript 13a

**P:** Pharmacist   **M:** Man

**1**

**P** Can I help you?

**M** Yes. Have you got anything for a headache?

**P** We've got aspirin or paracetamol.

**M** Er ... paracetamol, please.

**P** A large or a small bottle?

**M** How big are they?

**P** 50 tablets or 100 tablets.

**M** A small bottle then, please. And how many can I take?

**P** You can take two every four hours, if you need to. It's on the side of the bottle.

**M** Fine. Do I pay here?

**P** No. If you could take it to the cash desk over there, please ...

**2**

**P:** Pharmacist   **W:** Woman   **D:** Her daughter

**W** Do you have anything for sunburn – something to put on the skin? My daughter's burnt her arms and back quite badly.

**P** I see. Could I have a look at her arms?

**W** Yes, show the lady, Sophie.

**P** Um, yes, it is quite bad, isn't it?

**D** Mm.

**P** Well, I can give you some cream for burns, but there's not really much we can do now. The most important thing is to keep it covered up if you go out into the sun again.

**W** Yes, of course.

**P** And in future, remember to use a good sunscreen lotion. She's got very fair skin.

**W** Yes, she was very silly. And which cream do you recommend?

**P** This one's very good. You can use it as often as you want.

**W** Right, we'll take that one then. Thank you very much.

**3**

**P:** Pharmacist     **W:** Woman

**W** Erm . . . Excuse me.

**P** Yes?

**W** Er . . . Do you have anything for, er . . . diarrhoea?

**P** Is it for an adult?

**W** Er, yes. For my husband, actually.

**P** I see. And how bad is it?

**W** Well, quite bad, actually. Yes . . . all night.

**P** Any vomiting?

**W** No, no. Just the . . . er . . . you know . . .

**P** I see. Well, I can give you this. A spoonful of this medicine three times a day should help to stop the diarrhoea.

**W** Thanks.

**P** But if it's very bad I think he should see a doctor.

**W** Oh, we don't know a doctor here.

**P** Well, there's a phone number up there by the door, can you see? Really I think that's the best thing.

**W** Yes, I see. Well, where can I pay for the medicine . . .?

### Tapescript 13b

**1**

**P** Can I help you?

**M** Yes. Have you got anything for a headache?

**2**

**M** And how many can I take?

**P** You can take two every four hours, if you need to. It's on the side of the bottle.

**3**

**M** Fine. Do I pay here?

**P** No. If you could take it to the cash desk over there, please . . .

**4**

**W** My daughter's burnt her arms and back quite badly.

**P** I see. Could I have a look at her arms?

**W** Yes, show the lady, Sophie.

**5**

**W** And which cream do you recommend?

**P** This one's very good. You can use it as often as you want.

**6**

**W** Er . . . Do you have anything for, er . . . diarrhoea?

**P** Is it for an adult?

**W** Er, yes. For my husband, actually.

**7**

**P** I see. And how bad is it?

**W** Well, quite bad, actually. Yes . . . all night.

# Unit 14

### Tapescript 14a

**Debby** . . . no, sure I did. It's right here in my . . . Oh no! It's gone!

**Don** What? What's happened? What's the matter?

**Debby** My handbag! It's gone! I don't believe it!

**Don** Your handbag? Gee, where did you last have it?

**Debby** Um . . . I don't know. Um . . . I had it when we were in the café. In there, I guess.

**Don** Well, don't worry. What was in it? Can you remember?

**Debby** It had my passport and . . . oh, everything! This is awful!

**Don** Well, how about money? Was there any money in it?

**Debby** Uh, no, I don't think so. No, all my money's here, in my pocket.

**Don** Well, that's one thing . . .

**Debby** Yeah, but I had all my credit cards in there.

**Don** Oh, no!

**Debby** . . . and my driver's licence – that was in there.

**Don** Well, we can replace those.

**Debby** . . . and the traveller's cheques. Let's see. Did I have them in my handbag?

**Don** No, that's OK. I have the traveller's cheques right here. See? Well, listen, we'd better go back to the café, and go see if someone found it. You never know.

**Debby** No, I'll call them first. There's a telephone box right here.

**Don** OK.

**Debby** Oh! Can you lend me your phone card? Mine was in my handbag.

**Don** Yeah, sure. Here you are.

**Debby** Thanks. Well, let's hope . . .

### Tapescript 14b

**D:** Debby     **M:** Manageress of café

**M** Hello, Chestnut Tree Café.

**D** Hello. Um. My husband and I were in your café, um, about an hour ago, about 2.30.

**M** Yes?

**D** And . . . uh, we were sitting at a table in the corner, next to the door, right next to the door.

**M** Yes, table six.

**D** Well, I think I left my handbag on the table. Or maybe on the chair.

**M** Oh, I see.

**D** Did anyone hand it in?

**M** A handbag. What kind of handbag was it?

**D** It was a leather one.

**M** A leather handbag. Mm. And what did it look like?

**D** It's light brown – quite a small handbag. It had my passport – it's an American passport – in it and all my identification.

**M** I see. Well, I haven't seen any handbags. I'll just have a look to check.

**M** Hello?

**D** Hello.

**M** No, I'm sorry, there's nothing.

**D** Oh, no! Are you sure?

**M** Well, nobody's handed anything in.

**D** I see. Well, if you *do* find something, my name is Debby Knight. That's K-N-I-G-H-T.

**M** Yes.

**D** And I'm staying at the Victoria Hotel. The number is double-six eight seven eight.

**M** OK. Well, if we find it, we'll phone you.

**D** Thank you. It *is* very important.

**M** We will.

**D** OK. Thank you. Bye now.

**M** Bye.

### Tapescript 14c

1 Where did you last *have* it?
2 What *was* in it?
3 *Was* there any money in it?
4 What *did* it look like?
5 What kind of handbag *was* it?
6 Where did you *leave* it exactly?

# Unit 15

### Tapescript 15a

**M:** Marisol   **MB:** Mrs Burns

**MB** Did you find a school, Marisol?

**M** Well, I've got some adverts from the phone book.

**MB** Oh, yes? Anything good?

**M** Well, the first one I saw is called 'The Knightsbridge School of English'. That's in the centre of London, isn't it?

**MB** Yes, very near the centre anyway. But it says 'morning and afternoon', and you want evening, don't you?

**M** Mm. Well, there's this one, 'Living Languages'. It says 'Intensive and Examination courses'. I wonder if they do First Certificate?

**MB** Mm. Where is it exactly?

**M** It's in . . . Clapham.

**MB** Well, that's quite a long way from here. It's about 40 minutes by Underground.

**M** Oh, I think that's too far. How about this one? 'The English Studies Centre'. It's in Kensington. That's quite near, isn't it?

**MB** Yes, it's not far. You could go there by bus.

**M** Or there's this one, St Patrick's College, in Highgate.

**MB** Yes, that's *very* near. Well, why don't you give them both a ring? You can ask for some more information and practise your English at the same time.

**M** OK, I'll do it now. Now, where are the numbers?

### Tapescript 15b

**R:** Receptionist   **M:** Marisol

**R** St Patrick's College. Good afternoon.

**M** Hello. I'd like to know about your English courses. Do you have courses for the Cambridge First Certificate?

**R** Yes, we do. We have special courses for First Certificate and Proficiency.

**M** Ah, good! Could you tell me something about the courses? What time can I come to class?

**R** Well, there are full-time courses in the morning. That's every day from 9.00 to 12.00, or part-time in the evenings. That's 6.30 to 8.30, Tuesdays and Thursdays.

**M** Sorry, 6.30 to . . .?

**R** 6.30 to 8.30, Tuesday and Thursday evenings.

**M** I see. Could you tell me the price, please?

**R** Yes, our fees are £480 a month for the intensive courses, and £80 for the part-time courses.

**M** And how long does a course last?

**R** The full-time course lasts ten weeks, and the part-time course is eighteen weeks. The next course begins on the 28th of January.

**M** January . . . 28th . . . OK. Thank you. Oh, one more thing . . . How many students are there in a class?

**R** The maximum is twelve.

**M** OK, that's fine. Perhaps I'll come and see you tomorrow then.

**R** Certainly. Reception is open all day from 9.00 to 4.00.

**M** Thank you very much. Bye.

**R** Goodbye, and thank you for calling.

**Tapescript 15c**

**a. M** Do you have courses for the Cambridge First
Certificate?

   **R** Yes, we do. We have special courses for First Certificate
and Proficiency.

**b. M** What time can I come to class?

   **R** Well, there are full-time courses in the morning. That's
every day from 9.00 to 12.00, or part-time in the
evenings.

**c. M** I see. Could you tell me the price, please?

   **R** Our fees are £480 a month for the intensive courses,
and £80 for the part-time courses.

**d. M** And how long does a course last?

   **R** The full-time course lasts ten weeks, and the part-time
course is eighteen weeks.

**e. M** How many students are there in a class?

   **R** The maximum is twelve.

# Answer key

## Unit 1

**Listening for information**

### Nice to meet you

| Name | Marc | Maree |
|---|---|---|
| Nationality | Belgian | Australian |
| Destination after Paris | Brussels | back to London |
| Occupation | (university) student | teacher |
| In Paris for how long? | one night | two or three days |

**Listening for language**

**2**  1  *Where* are you from – England?
  2  Are you *staying* in Paris?
  3  *Are* you from Paris?
  4  What *do* you do?
  5  I'm sorry, I haven't *introduced* myself.
     My name's Marc.
  6  *Would* you like to come and have some
     breakfast?

No, actually. I'm *from* Australia.
Just for two or three *days*.
No, no. I'm not *French*.
I'm a *teacher*. I teach small children in a
primary school.
Nice to *meet* you, Marc.
Breakfast? Oh, yes! That would be *nice*.

## Unit 2

**Before you listen**

### In the air

**2**  1  You have a meal.            O
  2  You go through customs.        B/A
  3  You get off the plane.         A
  4  You check in your baggage.     B
  5  You take off.                  O
  6  You watch a video.             O
  7  You show your passport.        B/A
  8  You land.                      O
  9  You fasten your seat-belt.     O
  10  You collect your baggage.     A

**Listening for information**

1 Her name is Carmen Morales.
She's travelling to Miami *on business*.
She has *one child*.
She feels *calm*.
She *travels to Miami regularly*.
Her name is Audrey Wilkinson.
It's her *second* flight.
She's flying to Miami to see her *grandson*.
*He's two months* old.
She feels *excited*.

**Listening for language**

1 a. Check-in desk/ground staff
b. On the plane/cabin staff/pilot
c. On the plane/cabin staff
d. Check-in desk/ground staff
e. At customs/customs officer
f. On the plane/pilot
g. At the arrivals gate/the person meeting you
h. On the plane/check-in desk/cabin staff/ground staff

3 a. Same
b. Same
c. Different   *a drink*, not *something to drink*.
d. Different   *How many bags, please?* not *How many bags have you got, please?*
e. Different   *this suitcase*, not *these suitcases*.
f. Same
g. Different   *Did you have*, not *I hope you had*.
h. Different   *Have a comfortable*, not *good*.
(Although some sentences are different, they are all possible and correct!)

# Unit 3

## Everything you need to know

**Before you listen**

| 1 | 1 a post office | 2 a. buy | h. phone |
| | 2 a bus stop | b. phone | i. catch |
| | 3 a newsagent's | c. send/post | j. send/post/buy |
| | 4 a phone box | d. change/send | |
| | 5 a post box | e. buy | |
| | 6 a station | f. catch | |
| | 7 a bank | g. change/buy | |

3 Possible questions

Is there a | bank
phone box   near here?
etc.

Where is the nearest | bank
phone box   ?
etc.

Where can I find a ... ?
Can you tell me where the ... is?

**Listening for information**

**1** a.  a post box and the station

  b.  She wants to post some postcards to Turkey, and she wants to travel by train (early) tomorrow morning, so she thinks it's a good idea to find the station today.

**2** She is difficult to understand because she speaks quickly and she gives a lot of information all at the same time. She also has an accent (London).

**3** a., c., e., and f. should be ticked.

**Listening for language**

(See tapescript 3b for answers.)

**Speaking**

B's answers to A's questions.

A *How many books can I borrow?*

B  You can have three books for three weeks. If you have them for more than three weeks you have to pay a fine of thirty pence a week for every book.

A *What time does the library open and close every day?*

B  It opens at 9.00 every day from Monday to Saturday, and it closes at 8.00 every evening from Monday to Friday. On Saturday it closes at 5.00. It isn't open on Sundays.

A *Is there a quiet place where I can study?*

B  Yes, there's a reading room on the second floor. It's open from 10.00 to 5.00 every day, but it closes for lunch between 1.00 and 2.00 every day.

A *Where can I find Shakespeare's plays?*

B  Go through these doors, turn right and you will see some stairs in front of you. Go up the stairs and the Shakespeare section is on the right.

# Unit 4

# At the bank

**Listening for information**

**1** Picture a. Dialogue  2

    b.          4

    c.          1

    d.          5

    e.          3

**2** Dialogue 1  The customer wants to change $250 into £ sterling. He receives £140.

  Dialogue 2  The customer wants to cash a traveller's cheque for £100.

  Dialogue 3  The customer's name is De Oliveira.

  Dialogue 4  The customer needs his passport and a letter from his employer or place of study.

  Dialogue 5  The cashier gives the customer seven notes (3 × £20, 4 × £10).

**Listening for language**

**2** a.  I'd like to change this <u>into</u> pounds sterling, please.

  b.  I'd like to <u>cash</u> a traveller's cheque, please.

  c.  Can you <u>sign</u> here, please?

  d.  <u>Is</u> the money here?

  e.  I want <u>to open</u> a bank account here.

  f.  How <u>would</u> you like the money?

  g.  Can I <u>have</u> three twenty pound notes and four tens, please.

**3** The cashier says sentences c. and f.

  The customers says sentences a., b., d., e., and g.

# Unit 5

## Starting conversations

### Listening for information

**1**

| Relationship | Conversation about |
|---|---|
| 1 classmates/friends | (last) weekend |
| 2 business associates | woman's journey |
| 3 strangers | visiting/nationality/where from |
| 4 mother/son | film that son saw |
| 5 neighbours/friends | plans for weekend |
| 6 colleagues/friends | new pullover |

**2** a. The girl

b. (A cup of) coffee and a sandwich

c. Hamilton, in the south of Canada, near Toronto

d. It was all right. *The Lost Dream*

e. She's going to take her children to the seaside.

f. On Saturday, from a shop called 'Zed'

### Listening for language

**1** 1c.   2a.   3c.   4b.   5c.   6c.

# Unit 6

## Looking for somewhere to stay

### Before you listen

**2**

a. – a central position in the town

– they can pay by credit card

– they can have a private bathroom

b. They want to pay less than 200 francs a night

c. They want to stay for three nights.

**1**

### Listening for information

|  | Hotel Jungfrau | Hotel Montrose | Hotel Astoria |
|---|---|---|---|
| double room? | yes | yes | yes |
| bathroom? | yes | no | yes |
| three nights? | yes | no | yes |
| price? | 230 f | 150 f | 440 f |
| Access | no | ? | yes |

**Listening for language**

**1** See tapescript 6c for answers.

**Information for the receptionist at the Grand Victoria Hotel**

There are double rooms available with and without a private bathroom. With a private bathroom, a double room costs 290 francs. Without a bathroom, a double room costs 200 francs a night. You take all credit cards. There are rooms available for the next two, three, or four nights.

---

# Unit 7

# Going sightseeing

**Before you listen**

New York

**Listening for information**

**1** They talk about
  – The Empire State Building
  – The Statue of Liberty
  – The World Trade Center
  They also mention
  – The Guggenheim
  – The Museum of Modern Art

  – The Metropolitan Museum of Art
  – Central Park

  – Ellis Island

**2** Part 1 a. x   b. √   c. √     Part 2 a. x   b. x   c. x     Part 3 a. √   b. x   c. √   d. √

**Listening for language**

**1** 1d.  2f.  3a.  4b.  5c.  6e.
**2** 1A  2L  3L  4A  5A  6A
   a.A  b.L  c.L  d.L  e.L  f.A

---

# Unit 8

# At the travel agent's

**Listening for information**

**3** 1  Three
   2  £506
   3  £806
   4  The cheapest one (for £506)
   5  Tuesday, Thursday, and Saturday

   6  22
   7  Four hours
   8  Yes (It gets very full in summer.)
   9  £50
   10  Six weeks before he travels

**Listening for language**

**2** 1d.  2e.  3f.  4a.  5b.  6c.

---

# Unit 9

# In the pub

**Before you listen**

**3** 1  a half of bitter and a packet of crisps
   2  a half of lager and a packet of crisps
   3  a half of lager and a plate of chips
   4  a half of bitter
   5  a pint of bitter, a half of lager, and two packets of crisps
   6  a pint and a half of lager and a packet of crisps

| | |
|---|---|
| **Listening for information** | **1** a. 2  b. 4  c. 5 |
| **Listening for language** | **1/2** 1d.  2a.  3e.  4h.  5f.  6i.  7b.  8g.  9c. |

# Unit 10    Friends for dinner

**Before you listen**

**1** **Before you eat** Bring flowers/something to drink, prepare the food, offer to help in the kitchen, lay the table, offer something to drink.
**While you eat** Say something nice about the food, serve the food, offer something to drink.
**After you eat** Do the washing up, thank the hosts.

**Listening for information**

| In the picture | On the tape |
|---|---|
| 1 Anna is making the salad. | Bruce is making the salad. |
| 2 Fiona has the wine, Tom has the flowers. | Tom has the wine, Fiona has the flowers. |
| 3 Fiona is having red wine. | Fiona is drinking white wine. |
| 4 The main dish is fish. | The main dish is chicken. |
| 5 Anna is serving seconds to Fiona. | Fiona doesn't want any more/Tom has seconds. |
| 6 It's 11.15. | It's 12.15. |

**Note** The students aren't expected to produce full sentences. Notes are fine.

**Listening for language**

**1** a. Come in!   (H)
  b. Would you like something to drink?   (H)
  c. Do you need any help?   (G)
  d. Mm. That looks delicious!   (G)
  e. That was lovely!   (G)
  f. Would you like some more?   (H)
  g. Thank you for having us.   (G)

**2** a. Thanks.
  b. Yes, please.
  c. No, it's OK, thanks.
  d. I hope it is!
  e. Oh, thank you.
  f. No, thanks, really/Well, just a little, thanks.
  g. Thank *you* for coming.

# Unit 11    Hiring a car

**Before you listen**

**2** *VAT* is a tax on luxuries such as TVs or restaurant meals.
  **Unlimited mileage* means that it doesn't matter how many miles you travel – you pay the same. (1 mile = 1.7 kilometres)

**Listening for information**

**2** Number 3 is the correct note.

**Listening for language**

**1** a. 8  b. 5  c. 7  d. 8  e. 8 (counting EC as one word)
**2** (See tapescript 11b for missing words.)

## Unit 12     Going to the gym

**Listening for information**

**1** 1 Saturday     3 aerobics     5 £3.50
    2 12.30–1.30     4 advanced     6 evenings

**Listening for language**

**1** a. you     e. from     i. from     m. at
   b. some    f. to      j. to      n. in
   c. are     g. on     k. in      o. and
   d. a      h. an     l. the

## Unit 13     At the chemist's

**Before you listen**

**1**

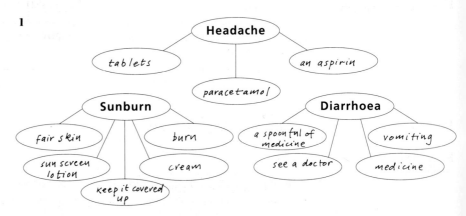

**2** vomiting /ˈvɒmɪtɪŋ/    tablets /ˈtæbləts/     a spoonful of medicine
medicine /ˈmedsən/      burn /bɜːn/        /əˈspuːnfʊl əv ˈmedsən/
aspirin /ˈæsprɪn/       paracetamol /pærəˈsetəmɒl/   cream /kriːm/
fair skin /feə ˈskɪn/     see a doctor /siː ə dɒktə/    sunscreen lotion
keep it covered up /kiːpɪt kʌvəd ˈʌp/             /ˈsʌnskriːn ləʊʃən/

**Listening for information**

**1** Headache     Sunburn       Diarrhoea
  1 aspirin      1 burn         1 vomiting
  2 paracetamol   2 cream        2 a spoonful of (this) medicine
  3 tablets      3 keep it covered up   3 see a doctor
             4 sunscreen lotion    4 medicine
             5 fair skin

**2** 1 a. We don't know – probably himself.
    b. A bottle of 50 paracetamol
    c. No
  2 a. The woman's daughter
    b. Some cream for burns
    c. Keep it covered up/Next time use sunscreen lotion.
  3 a. The woman's husband
    b. Some medicine for diarrhoea
    c. Her husband should see a doctor.

**Listening for language**

**1** 1a. 2b. 3a. 4b. 5a. 6b. 7b.

# Unit 14        Lost and found

**Listening for information**

**1** a. Pictures 1, 2, 4, and 5 should be ticked.

    b. She thinks she left her handbag in the café.

    c. They decide to telephone the café to see if the handbag has been handed in.

**2** Time lost:             2.30 approx.

    **Where sitting:**     in the corner/next to the door/table six

    **Description:**        colour – light brown

                      material – leather

                      size – quite small

    **If found please phone:**   Debby Knight/Victoria Hotel

    **Telephone:**        66878

**Listening for language**

**1**  1  Where did you last *have* it?

    2  What *was* in it?

    3  *Was* there any money in it?

    4  What *did* it look like?

    5  What kind of handbag *was it*?

    6  Where did you *leave* it exactly?

**2**  1f.  2e.  3b.  4d.  5c.  6a.

# Unit 15        Choosing an English course

**Before you listen**

**3**  School

    1  offers courses for just a few hours a week.

    *3*  tells you the dates when courses begin.

    2  tells you how many students there are in a class.

    2  *doesn't* mention exam classes.

    4  gives the price of courses.

    3  tells you what time the classes start/finish.

**Listening for information**

**1**

| English Studies Centre | | Knightsbridge School of English | | Living Languages | | St Patrick's College | |
|---|---|---|---|---|---|---|---|
| | √ | | | | | | √ |

**2** One school provided morning and afternoon classes, but not evening classes. The other was too far away.

**3**

> First Cert: Yes
> Times:   9.00–12.00 6.30–8.30
> Days of part-time course: Tuesdays and Thursdays
> Fees: £480 full-time/£80 part-time
> No. of weeks: 10 weeks full-time/18 weeks part-time
> No. of students per class: 12

**Listening for language**

**2** Marisol's questions:
   a. Do you have courses for the Cambridge First Certificate?
   b. What time can I come to class?
   c. Could you tell me the price, please?
   d. How long does a course last?
   e. How many students are there in a class?

# JUBILEE SPORTS CENTRE

≈≈≈≈≈≈≈

## SWIMMING POOL

### OPENING TIMES

| | |
|---|---|
| MONDAY | 12.30 - 8.00 |
| TUESDAY | 12.30 - 8.00 |
| WEDNESDAY | 12.30 - 10.00 |
| THURSDAY | 12.30 - 8.00 |
| FRIDAY | 12.30 - 8.00 |
| SATURDAY | 9.30 - 6.30 |
| SUNDAY | 9.30 - 5.30 |

### PRICES

ADULTS: £1.75          CHILDREN: 75P

≈≈≈≈≈≈≈

## SAUNA

| | |
|---|---|
| OPEN EVERY DAY | 2.00 - 5.30 |
| PRICE | £2.00 PER HALF HOUR |

# JUBILEE SPORTS CENTRE

∞∞∞∞∞∞∞∞∞∞∞

## Y O G A

| DAY | TIME | LEVEL | PRICE |
|---|---|---|---|
| 1 MON/WED | 6.30 - 8.00 | BEGINNER | £3.00 |
| 2 TUES/THURS | 6.30 - 8.00 | BEGINNER | £3.00 |
| 3 TUES/THURS | 6.30 - 8.00 | INTERMEDIATE/ADVANCED | £3.00 |